The Cambridge Manuals of Science and
Literature

ECONOMICS AND SYNDICALISM

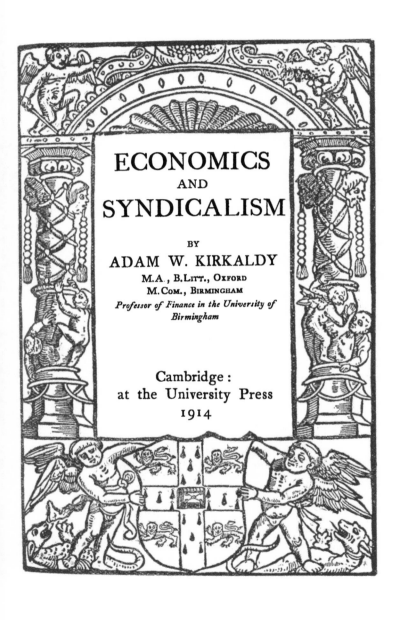

ECONOMICS
AND
SYNDICALISM

BY

ADAM W. KIRKALDY

M.A., B.LITT., OXFORD
M.COM., BIRMINGHAM

*Professor of Finance in the University of
Birmingham*

Cambridge :
at the University Press
1914

CAMBRIDGE UNIVERSITY PRESS
Cambridge, New York, Melbourne, Madrid, Cape Town,
Singapore, São Paulo, Delhi, Tokyo, Mexico City

Cambridge University Press
The Edinburgh Building, Cambridge CB2 8RU, UK

Published in the United States of America by Cambridge University Press, New Yo

www.cambridge.org
Information on this title: www.cambridge.org/9781107646650

© Cambridge University Press 1914

First published 1914
First paperback edition 2011

A catalogue record for this publication is available from the British Library

ISBN 978-1-107-64665-0 Paperback

*With the exception of the coat of arms at
the foot, the design on the title page is a
reproduction of one used by the earliest known
Cambridge printer, John Siberch, 1521*

TO

E. F. K.

PREFACE

THE Industrial World is passing through a stage of acute unrest. The situation has not developed suddenly, nor was it unexpected by those who know what has been going on quietly for some years past.

Pamphlets and leaflets dealing with industrial questions, wages, employment, profits, the wrongs of the workers, the oppression of the employers, have been written by men having a grievance against society, or in some cases by clever men eager to lead their readers astray, and to do so of set purpose. These publications have had a wide circulation among the working classes. Many of them are written in an interesting form, and contain half-truths speciously dressed up to resemble facts. They have gradually worked their way, until having for the most part been left uncontradicted, hundreds of working men have accepted their teachings as proved. And now the seed having been sown, the reaping of the whirlwind has commenced.

The object of this little book is to draw attention to some points of special interest at the present moment. It is by no means too late for the back-

bone of the industrial army to adopt an attitude on
economic questions which will make for evolution
and progress instead of revolution and disaster.   The
chief mischief is wrought by ignorance, or by a partial consideration of the natural laws which regulate
the industrial sphere.   The economists of the early
nineteenth century made the mistake of concentrating too much on the production of wealth.
Then arose theorists who showed the economist his
error, and it was made plain, that not only how
to produce wealth to the best advantage and in
the greatest amount should be studied, but how
wealth when produced should be distributed among
the factors co-operating in its production.   Unhappily extremists have fallen into the error of
concentrating their attention on the question of distribution ;   and this has led to what is called the
ca' canny policy.   Some leaders ignore the fact that
labour of all grades is paid out of what it produces,
not out of some existing fund.   Rising prices are
due to a great extent to the fact that with higher
wages and shorter hours there is a smaller output per
unit, to some extent caused either directly or indirectly by this policy.   Under such circumstances
higher wages cannot benefit the working man.
What is needed at the present moment is that all
ranks in the industrial army should be equally well
versed in the economic laws which regulate, not only

the *production of wealth*, but also its *distribution* and its *consumption*.   Until this comes about society will continue to grope in the dark, and there will be not only unrest, but the possibility of worse things.

It is a most hopeful sign that the more serious sections of the working classes are striving after a real knowledge of economic laws and their working.

I would take this opportunity to thank Mr W. J. Davis, President of the Trade Union Congress, for his ready permission to print the speeches of the French and German Delegates at the Manchester meeting.   These speeches speak for themselves. May the time never come when English working men as a body shall accept the opinion that the advancement of their interests depends on a warfare between wage-earners on the one hand and the employing-class and the State on the other !   The acceptance of such teaching can only lead to one result—disaster.

A. W. K.

March 1914.

CONTENTS

APPENDICES

BOOKS TO CONSULT

Sir Arthur Clay. Syndicalism and Labour. John Murray. London. 1912. 1s.

Louis Levine, Ph.D. The Labour Movement in France. (A Study in Revolutionary Syndicalism.) Columbia University. 1912. $1.50

J. Ramsay Macdonald, M.P. Syndicalism. (A Critical Examination.) Constable & Co. London. 1s.

Philip Snowden, M.P. The Living Wage. Hodder & Stoughton. London. 1s.

Philip Snowden, M.P. Socialism and Syndicalism. Collins. London. 1s.

The Miners' Next Step. (Issued by the Unofficial Reform Committee.) Robert Davies & Co. Tonypandy. 1912.

ECONOMICS
AND SYNDICALISM

CHAPTER I

UNCONSCIOUS AND SEMI-CONSCIOUS ECONOMISTS

To understand the present economic situation, the outcome of which appears to so many people to have resolved itself into an alternative, either socialism or syndicalism, it is necessary to have at least a bowing acquaintance with the development of economic theory and practice from the earliest days. These have really developed as man himself has progressed.

During the period which is known as ancient history, the economist was unconscious; during that period which is roughly termed the Middle Ages, he may be called semi-conscious. It was not until about the middle of the seventeenth century that thinking man became conscious that there was a science of economics, and began to make efforts towards unravelling its laws, and understanding its tendencies,

A

In this country two great economic events mark
the time when the conscious economist appeared
upon the scene. At that time England was engaged
in wresting from Holland the supremacy in foreign
trade and shipping, which the Dutch had taken from
the Portuguese. During the time that Amsterdam
was the economic centre of the trading community,
the great Bank had been founded which had proved
of enormous benefit to both local and international
business. From the experience of this Bank important lessons as to banking and currency had
been learned—indeed, it may be said that this
great institution, although its organisation was by
no means perfect, marks an epoch in commercial
history—namely, the inauguration of modern banking. As the English began to compete successfully
with the Dutch for foreign trade, and London began
to take the place of Amsterdam as the great commercial centre, there were vague suggestions that a
Bank of London should be founded. But until
William Paterson propounded his scheme for the
establishment of a Bank of England, the suggestions
failed to take form. For three years after its
promulgation Paterson's scheme remained almost
unheeded, but in 1694, mainly owing to the exigencies
of the political situation, the Bank of England was
founded. Two years later a recoinage was carried
through in England, and round these two events a

very interesting controversy raged, which gave rise
to the writing of a considerable number of pamphlets
and books, in some of which it is quite evident the
writers were beginning to get glimmerings of economic
truth.   At any rate it is safe to say that about this
time there was a definite attempt in England to
formulate a science of economics.

But since both existing customs and prejudices
prove that the unconscious or semi-conscious theories
of ages long past continue to have an influence over
the material world, centuries after their *raison
d'être* has ceased, it is not only interesting but
necessary, in order to get a real understanding of
present-day thought, to trace down, even though it
only be possible to do so somewhat sketchily, some
of the main thoughts connected with economic
theory and practice from ancient days.

Roughly speaking, there have been four great
stages in human development.

I. *The Hunting Stage.*—Primitive man was a
hunter.   There were some wild fruits doubtless, but
man's food and clothing would consist for the most
part of the results of the chase.   It must have been
a very hard life, for until he devised them, man had
no weapons wherewith to hunt and kill the animals
he required for food.   But the economic situation
was a very simple one.   There being no private
property in land, there was no rent ; and as capital

only existed in a very rudimentary form, no question would arise as to what interest should be paid. As, however, man progressed, he furnished himself, as we know, with rude tools and weapons, the beginnings of capital, and doubtless he would use surplus skins and surplus flesh for exchange purposes. There even may have been, as time progressed, a rough and ready kind of currency, but taken as a whole, the economic situation was simple, and as such it has had but little effect on succeeding generations.

II. *The Pastoral Stage.*—As time went on man developed new resources ; he found it possible to domesticate certain animals ; he would capture the young, or take care of the weakly or slightly injured, and find that in some instances they were tameable. At any rate, we know that from the hunting stage man entered upon what is called the pastoral stage, and at this juncture he became a shepherd, enjoying a far higher state of existence. Thus the pastoral stage is the second great stage in human development. Here the economic situation developed somewhat, but on the whole it remained simple. Either slavery or service was instituted, and there may ·have been, and doubtless was, a wages question. There was land ownership on a small scale, if only for burial purposes, as one may learn from the history of the Patriarchs in the Book of Genesis. The flocks and herds which these nomad shepherds collected were personal property, but pasturage was sought by wandering about from district to district, and there was but little thought of permanent settlement.

III. *The Agricultural Stage.*—Progress continued and eventually settlement began to take place, and mankind passed from the pastoral to the agricultural stage. In this the economic situation developed in many new and interesting directions. In order to practise the arts of agriculture, it was necessary that settlement, including land ownership, or at least security of tenure, should be practised, and so we find man clearing the land and producing new and improved crops, carrying on side by side, each assisting the other, pastoral and agricultural pursuits ; a very healthy and a very interesting stage of existence, which apparently mankind was loath to leave.

But progress, although perhaps imperceptible to the man on the spot, continued working in the village communities, which gradually developed in connection with agriculture. In these, moreover, separation of employments was found to give advantages so great, that as time went on each little village had its own wheelwright, carpenter, smith, and other separate tradesmen. The market for which these men worked was known and well-defined ; it consisted of the requirements of the little, self-contained community in the midst of which the lot of these artificers was thrown.

IV. *The Commercial and Industrial Stage.*—As centuries passed, these communities developed, and their needs increased ; the simple food, clothing, housing, and amusements of early days no longer sufficed. With improved methods of agriculture, and improved tools for manufacturing articles required by an agricultural community, the men practising separate employments increased their output, with the result that they sought a wider market. In other words, the agricultural stage reached its highest point, and a new era opened out before the progressive man. This is known as the commercial and industrial stage. This stage has continued down to the present time, though it too has been subject to development since the comparatively simple beginnings made in the agricultural village or small town. There was a great advance when what is known as the Guild System began to be practised. This system had, in its day, a very great and widespread influence on mankind. But it tended, as a system, to become petrified and inelastic, and with growing ideas concerning liberty, man became dissatisfied, and refused to be bound by archaic Guild Law. Fortunately this Guild Law only ran within certain limits, and so the progressive man went beyond these limits and commenced manufacturing and trading on a new system. Thus the Guild System gave place to the Domestic System. So long as tools were simple, and raw material was only required in comparatively small quantities, cottage industries could be practised with advantage, and the factor could go round collecting what had been manufactured in this comparatively retail way. The Domestic System had much to commend it. The worker on the whole lived a reasonable and happy existence ; but with invention and discovery, the limits of the market were still further widened, and with international demand, the Domestic System was unable satisfactorily to cope. With the invention of the steam engine and a number of rapidly working machines, the output of a given district could be enormously increased. But at this juncture another phenomenon emerged. With simple tools and a small demand, a scattered population could produce the several commodities required by the market. But for the successful application of steam power it became necessary that as many machines as possible should be run by one engine. Hence the invention of the steam engine brought about what is known as the *Industrial Revolution*, and the Industrial Revolution brought into existence the manufacturing town with its teeming population, and the many attendant problems.

Now this very sketchily and very roughly traces out centuries of growth; but the sketch is perhaps sufficient for the immediate purpose. Throughout all these stages there had been progress, as has been shown, and this progress was always due to some long-headed man or group of men. These men, desiring an enlargement of their life, and keenly anxious to make the most of their opportunities, had the effect of improving and broadening life for the whole of their fellows. These long-headed men were really economists. In the early stages of existence they were so unconsciously; they gradually became semi-conscious of economic possibilities, until with the developments that came at the end of the seventeenth century, full consciousness began to dawn.

It is of interest to realise that all these stages, which have been briefly described, exist to-day contemporaneously and can be studied from actual life. In North America and other parts of the world, some men are still in the hunting stage. In Asia and Africa, the shepherd can still be seen following his calling in much the same way as Abraham, Isaac, and Jacob. Primitive agriculture is still practised in various parts of the world, whilst incipient industries and the beginnings of commerce can be studied in more than one country.

Man has progressed through all the stages that

have been mentioned, and in each stage there can be traced both an economic theory and an economic practice. There have been laws and customs which not only regulated the society of the day, but many of them have continued to influence mankind down to the present time. It will be of interest to take one or two instances of old-world theories and practices which have very materially affected subsequent history.

India, Palestine, and Greece all furnish instances of ancient economic theory and practice which have had momentous effects on the economic history of the world. Money was considered to have peculiar powers inherent in it, and as in ancient days borrowers were usually people who were in some trouble, more or less temporary, it was considered that to take interest or usury for the use of a money loan was taking advantage of a poor man's necessity. And further than this, Aristotle definitely taught that, the precious metals being sterile substances, to pay interest on a money loan was unnatural ; that whilst there was natural increase in the case of the use of an orchard, or a herd of cattle, or a flock of sheep, for a given period (an increase which could be divided between the owner and the borrower), there was no special increase in the case of a loan of metal. In the Vedas, the Brahman was only allowed to take interest from a

wicked person. The teaching of Moses upon this
subject contains a very important modification
which is not found elsewhere ; for while he would
not permit a Jew to exact usury from a brother
Jew, he was careful to add that this law should
not apply to any business relations between Jew
and Gentile. This exception has indeed had great
consequences. When during the Middle Ages the
Church, in pursuit of the grandest possible ideal,
attempted to set up on earth a true Kingdom of
God, the Canon Law was gradually promulgated
with the object of regulating the conduct of mankind both in the spiritual and the material sphere.
This Law contains an economic theory, and on the
subject of payment of interest on money loans, the
reverend authors of the Law apparently forgot their
Old Testament and remembered Aristotle, for they
altogether prohibited the payment or exaction of
usury for a money loan. Hence, when trade and
commerce began to develop, the commercial community in Europe found itself sadly hampered by
this provision of the Canon Law. Fortunately,
however, by, on the one hand, making use of fictions,
and on the other, taking advantage of the prophetic
foresight of Moses, the difficulty was circumvented,
for whilst the Jews were prevented from following
a number of trades and professions, there was one
occupation which their Law and the Canon Law

left open to them. The Jew, for a time, was the
only man who legally and morally could exact
interest on a money loan, and so he became the
great banker and financier of the world. The ex-
ceedingly useful and foreseeing modification allowed
by Moses in an otherwise stringent and drastic
law has thus had the greatest possible consequences
on the financial and commercial history of the
world right down to the present moment.

Again, ancient politics were to a great extent
based on slavery. It is true that bond service has
passed away, but the effects of the teaching and
practice of these early days has continued to exert
its influence to the present moment. Trade and
business, manufacture and commerce, were looked
upon as unworthy occupations for a man of citizen
rank. The citizen might be an agriculturist, an
administrator, or a soldier, but he must not soil his
fingers with trade, and so these occupations, looked
upon with scorn by the citizens, were exercised by
the servile class. It is needless to say that this
class, deprived of the possibility of broadening their
outlook and humanising their intellects with culture
and education, developed qualities which tended to
increase still further the scorn with which the
citizen regarded them. Labour was degraded, the
producers were cut off from intellectual pursuits
and excluded from public life, and this for centuries

militated against industrial progress. As a direct result of old-world conditions, the Canon Law definitely stated that trade will lead to fraud, and that the only lawful occupations for the Christian man are agriculture or its simple attendant handicrafts. To make a long story short, the effect of this old teaching and practice still lingers, and is seen to-day in the class feeling which exists, though happily not so strongly as it did, between the professional man, the soldier, the administrator, and the tradesman.

As mankind developed new and higher activities the State emerged, and with the evolution of man, living in an organised and regulated community, the economic position becomes increasingly interesting. Ancient writers have a great deal to say about the circumstances which led to the foundation of the State, and from their works much can be learnt that helps one to picture the condition of society in these early organised communities, and as to the old-world conception of the duties and responsibilities of the citizen. For instance, Plato tells us that the State arises out of the needs of mankind, that no man is self-sufficing, for all of us have many wants. That having all these wants, and many people being necessary to supply them, the various individuals required for these many purposes gather themselves together as helpers or partners. This body of people is called a State. The individual members of which it is composed, exchange with each other—one gives, another receives—and the result is that these mutual exchanges confer a mutual benefit.

Thus the origin of the State is attributed to want of self-sufficiency on the part of the individual, together with advantages accruing from a separation of occupations, rendered possible by the establishment of a satisfactory system of exchange. This marks a very important advance indeed in economics, for the acknowledgment of the advantages connected with the separation of employments foreshadows the advantages which have accrued to mankind from the modern teaching and practice connected with division of labour, and although ancient philosophers never advanced to this point, they had, in grasping the advantages of separation of employments, travelled a long way along the road of economic science. Aristotle puts the matter somewhat differently, but practically means the same thing : ἄνθρωπος φύσει πολιτικὸν ζῷον —Man is essentially a social animal ; he loves company, and cannot attain to his highest in a solitary condition. The origin of the State is the family. For, as Aristotle puts it, man and woman cannot exist independently, and the association naturally formed for the supply of everyday wants, forms a household, whose members eat of one store. Then as the number of families increases, there arises the separation of occupations to which reference has just been made. This opens up possibilities for many uses and abuses of the economic position. For a time man may rest content with working to supply the daily needs of himself and those dependent on him, but a time comes when, while some men may go on doing this, and so practise what Aristotle calls *economics*, another and more pushing set of men will begin to strive after accumulations of wealth. The former is natural, the latter unnatural. Everything has a use and a misuse. To use a thing rightly is natural and proper, but to abuse it is unnatural. Thus Aristotle calls this unnatural use of wealth Chrematistics. Economics and chrematistics have something in common, at least there is an overlapping of their spheres. For included in the sphere of economics or household management come the production of those things needful for the due development of life, and the rules guiding their consumption. Moreover, as man is no longer a self-sufficing unit, exchange of simple superfluities in order to obtain a fuller life is lawful. But both the barter, or exchange and production of the necessaries of life, fall also within the sphere of chrematistics, or unnatural economics, for by increasing the amount of barter which supplies things needed for a fuller, yet still lawful style of life, one begins to practise money-making, and allied to this are efforts at an increased and unhealthy production of goods for the mere purpose of accumulating wealth. Hence, says Aristotle, while simple barter for one's needs is lawful, retail trading becomes more and more unnatural, because men continue to exchange after they have enough.

Returning for a moment to the question of expedient and inexpedient occupations, we learn that agriculture and pastoral pursuits are natural, whilst those connected with exchange and commerce are unnatural. Even here there is an overlapping in the natural and unnatural spheres, because mining and forestry may be included in either or both. This part of the subject should be noted, because one of the reasons why Aristotle takes up this attitude on the subject of trade is so frequently overlooked; the Canon Lawyers evidently passed it by unnoticed. For Aristotle taught that in the best government, where the citizens are all virtuous and happy, none of them should be permitted to exercise any low mechanical employment or traffic, for these are ignoble and destructive of virtue. At this point the quotation usually stops, but by reading on it will be seen that Aristotle had good reasons for his dictum; for he goes on to say that those destined for public office should not even be husbandmen, for leisure is necessary in order that the citizen may improve in virtue, and fulfil his duty to the State. Here both directly and indirectly is taught a great and much-needed lesson to modern democracy. Not only is there a justification for a reduction of working hours so that the citizen may have the leisure that is necessary if he is to grow in virtue, but if the vote is to be used intelligently and rightly, if the enfranchised portions of the community are to exercise their duties as citizens rightly, they must have a due limitation of the working day. This teaching does not give any support to the idler or the loafer. The citizen must work while he works, but neither the work, nor the hours occupied by the work, should be so exhausting, or so long, as to stunt a man's individuality and render him an unintelligent citizen.

The powerful influence exercised by the theories and practices of the ancient world on succeeding generations is recognised by every careful reader of history. In the following chapter will be traced out the course of events as Europe became Christianised and as the commercial stage was entered upon and passed through its various developments.

CHAPTER II

THE EFFECT OF NATIONALITY ON ECONOMIC THOUGHT AND PRACTICE

In the last chapter reference has been made to the teaching of the Mediæval Church on the subject of usury, and the rightful occupations for Christian people. The Corpus of Canon Law is well worthy of study, for that part of it which more especially affects this subject—namely, the regulations framed for the economic sphere—is of exceeding interest. To mention but a few points, the Church Lawyers held that community of goods, whereby the primary needs of all may be supplied, is theoretically right. The primitive disciples had not only taught but had practised this. Subsequent history, however, had seen the re-introduction of the system of private property, society was once again securely established on this practice, and naturally the question was raised—could it be said that Christianity had been subverted in this particular ? Here the Church legist borrowed a most convenient method of procedure from the juris-consult. Theoretically the hard and fast lines of the Roman Law could not be either changed or relaxed even in the slightest

B   17

degree. But the lawyer was equal to the occasion.
If facts are too strong, invent a fiction. And as the
Civil Law had been subject to amendment and
modernisation by means of fictions, so now the
definite practices of the early Church, which had
become difficult, if not impossible, to enforce in a
semi-heathen community, were softened down by
means of fictions. Community of goods is theoretically right, but the institution of private property
is a necessity owing to *man's fall*. The exacting
of usury on loans of money was absolutely forbidden,
as was also the exaction of a price fixed by the
haggling of the market. The seller, it was laid
down, must sell at *justum pretium*, and not at what
might be a momentarily fictitious value fixed by
supply and demand. The poor and needy *must* be
relieved ; this was no matter of mere choice and
philanthropy, but a legal debt—*debitum legale*.
The man who, in his business or other avocations,
practised the unnatural economics, was called an
avaricious man ; nor was there any shade of difference between the devotee of chrematistics and the
devotee of idols. An avaricious man, said the
Church, is an idolater.

From these few dicta it will be realised that the
ideal was high and noble, perhaps in its entirety
one of the noblest ever set up in this world ; but
whilst it might have been practised under more

primitive conditions with advantage, when applied to Europe at the moment when commercial developments were becoming more and more practical politics, such teaching, especially when enforced by an authority which wielded power, not only in this world, but in that to come, threatened to prove an impassable obstacle in the road of progress. Clerics did not realise that the world had not only changed, but was refusing to remain unprogressive. Theories and regulations which met the needs of the hunter and the shepherd were out of date. The infant mankind was growing up, and to attempt to keep the limbs of the stalwart and developing youth cramped within swaddling clothes would create a situation of disaster, either by repressing natural growth, or by causing the infant garments to burst. Nor is this lesson one that can be disregarded at the present moment. Each generation has its needs, and has to make its own way along the road of progress. To enjoy to the full the possibilities belonging to its epoch, whilst not in a revolutionary spirit disregarding all that is old, nor abolishing every law or custom handed down by preceding generations, it behoves it to realise its powers, its privileges, and its responsibilities. Thus the great aim should always be so to modify old laws and customs as to bring them into conformity with modern needs. The greatest lesson taught by history to the statesman, the lawyer, and the social reformer alike, is that in order to progress naturally—and that is synonymous with saying, in order that humanity may enjoy to the full the possibilities of the moment—there must be evolution, not revolution. The evolution must be natural, progressive, and healthy, because when this natural evolution is working, society advances with the times, but anything that tends to clog or obstruct a natural evolution inevitably decreases the pace, whilst blind revolutionary measures merely serve to put back the clock altogether.

One of the first lessons that has to be learned in political or social science, is that there has been throughout the ages *continuity*. This must be realised in all its bearings if progress is to be maintained. The natural sequences should be followed, and so far as it is possible for human statesmanship to grasp the great lessons of the past, they should be applied to the needs of the present, in order that the future may not be prejudiced, and human progress stultified by a break in evolution, which can only resemble the shunting of an express train on to a siding.

In the early Middle Ages Rome symbolised Unity, both ecclesiastical and political. The spiritual descendant of St Peter, as Bishop of Rome, was looked upon as the representative of God upon earth, and the Vicar of Christ. He was the Head of the Church, and as such ruled not only the souls of the faithful, but had a power, somewhat difficult for us to realise now, over all human concerns. Standing by the side of the Pope, but a step lower, came the Holy Roman Emperor, the secular head of society. Theoretically the Emperor was in the temporal sphere supreme. Beneath these two imposing figures society was divided up horizontally. Pope and Emperor each supreme in his proper sphere, then came the great officers in Church and State, Archbishops, Bishops, Abbots, Kings, Dukes, Earls, and so on down to clergy and laymen, the latter commencing with the lesser nobility and ending with the serf. There was hardly a trace of nationality. Europe had become cosmopolitan : but the seeds of disintegration were there, and were as time went on being sown more and more widely. The early Norman kings of England struck a chord which was to reverberate throughout the Continent when once the sun of progress began to quicken the good seed. On his accession, William the Conqueror only admitted with qualifications, the papal claims to jurisdiction over the English Church, nor was he a servile vassal of either his nominal feudal overlord, the King of France, or the Emperor, whose paper titles entitled him to a subservience almost equal to that accorded to the Deity Himself. The weak

spot in this organisation was that there were only
two positions of the first rank—one in the Church
and one in the State. With a feudal system breed-
ing men of virile action and independent thought, it
was not to be expected that only two positions of
splendour would be sufficient. Human ambition
is a powerful impulse, and it proved sufficient to
break down the system which in theory was well
fitted for the right governance of the world in
both the spiritual and material spheres. Ambitious
men may be content with such a system if they be
Pope or Emperor, but there being more ambitious
men than available positions, schisms arose in the
Church, as a result of which two or more individuals
claimed to be the representative of St Peter, and
called upon the faithful for their allegiance ; whilst
the Imperial position became a mere title to which
Europe paid but scant attention.

Among these various and contending forces a
great movement gradually took form, and with
what has been called the *Renaissance*, there was not
only a rebirth of learning and liberty, but from the
point of view now under consideration, something
far more momentous. With the *Renaissance* came
a rearrangement of society, for *Nationality* was the
greatest outcome of this rebirth. Europe became
divided up into constituent parts, and each of these
bound together by ties of race, speech, or tradition,

became a nation. In other words, the horizontal division of society proved to have been too artificial, and henceforward a vertical division, resulting from nationality, vitalised Europe with an *esprit* engendering a competition between State and State which, while entailing much that is regrettable, has powerfully affected the world for good. The attempts of recent years once again to make Europe cosmopolitan, the internationalisation of Socialism by Karl Marx and his followers, do not make for progress, for if successful they would tend to reproduce in the highest spheres, the petrifaction and lethargy which a healthier spirit fought against and conquered centuries ago. It may be conceded that conflicts of armies are a relic of barbarism, and should belong to past history, but twentieth century civilisation can only be quickened and be effective and progressive under the stimulus of a rivalry in the more peaceful spheres of science, invention, commerce, and industry. In these, individual, personal, and national characteristics have played, and continue to play, a healthy rôle, and are the mainspring of the clock of progress. But it may be asked how did the ideals of nationality affect economic thought and practice ? To answer this question a short excursion must be made into the domain of history in order to show how the earliest economic policy, definitely pursued and developed of set purpose by Government, originated. This policy is known as the Mercantile System, or Policy of Power. Its commencement is not altogether easy to trace, but it reached its highest development under Cromwell. Its inception was very largely due to a growing conception of nationality, and the ambition of some of our kings to increase alike their importance and their realm by carrying on a spirited foreign policy.

When the Anglo-Saxons conquered this country, and Britain became England, the kings, whether of the Heptarchy or following them, the kings of a united England, were expected to live of their own. This *own* consisted of the Royal Demesne, lands set apart for the king, into which the spare land of the community became absorbed. Early English kings were great landowners, but their estates were hardly private property, for their revenues were expected to be sufficient to carry on the work of government and support the royal dignity.

The Northmen invasions, however, led to an important modification in this simple system. Weak kings commenced a system of bribing the Northmen either to go or to keep away. These bribes were mainly paid in money or valuables, and to raise the necessary sums taxes were levied. The history of taxation in this country is full of interest, for some of our most highly prized liberties were won by means of bargaining between people and Government. Had the revenue of the Royal Demesne continued to be sufficient to meet the needs of the Government, in all human probability our monarchy would have been autocratic, and our liberties very considerably circumscribed.

As the nation progressed, however, it was no longer possible for a king to live of his own, and the necessity for levying money taxes increased. This tendency was subject to a remarkable development under some of our most notable kings. Henry II., Edward I., and Edward III. all required large amounts of additional revenue to enable them to follow their ambitions. In very early days experience had taught the difficulty of exacting money from the agricultural interest, but as towns and cities began to flourish, the Government discovered that there was a fund of wealth being created by traders and manufacturers from which the sinews of war could be extracted. Hence it became an important aim of the Government to foster trade and manufactures, not because these pursuits were loved for their own sakes, but because by means of them a very valuable taxable fund might be built up. From this evolved the Mercantile System which became the economic policy of Western Europe from the break up of the mediæval system.

There are some points of resemblance between the
Mercantile System and State Socialism. Both
have as a common ideal the State organised on an
industrial and commercial basis. It is in their
ultimate aims that they differ ; for while the
Mercantilist strove after national self-sufficiency,
the aim of the State Socialist is that, by means of
State ownership of all the means and factors of
production, every child born into the community
may have a level chance in life.

The Mercantile System, in its most developed
form, imposed upon this country a corpus of legisla-
tion whose object was the building up of a great
and wealthy State. This included the Navigation
Laws, the first of which dates from the reign of
Richard II., whilst the final form was due to the
genius of Cromwell. These laws had as their
definite object the creation of a great . mercantile
marine. Another great feature of the policy was
the Corn Laws, whose object it was to protect and
help farmers, so that England might be independent
of supplies of grain from abroad ; there were also
the Statutes of Apprentices, and the Poor Law
framed to regulate the labour force, and to deal
with the problem of poverty.

Great men evolved a great policy under which
a great empire and a great commerce were successfully founded. Smaller men carried the policy

to excess ; they did not realise that a scaffolding may be necessary for the construction of a building, but that it would be mere folly to keep the scaffolding in place after the building has been completed. The Mercantile System became petrified and inelastic ; its supporters looked upon it as a permanent part of the constitution, which must not be modified in any particular. The great aim of Government, they said, was to foster a favourable balance of trade ; to this end exports must exceed imports in value, so that the balance might be received in gold. This created a very interesting situation which, but for the good sense of leading men, might have entailed commercial and political decay. Fortunately, however, at the moment when the policy appeared to be most solidly established, men with large views, and a more than ordinary foresight, began to question its permanent utility, and to fathom some of the delusions dear to its advocates. Men like Sir William Petty and Sir Dudley North not only realised that the old system was getting outworn, that the building having been built the scaffolding should be removed, but they began to formulate a new policy to meet the changed conditions of the economic sphere. Their theories are the beginning of those doctrines of natural liberty which were perfected a century later by Adam Smith. The steps by which these new doctrines evolved may be briefly stated. Originating in England, they found their way to France and led to further speculations. The new theories brought about the formation of a new school of economic thinkers, known as the Physiocrats. These men, inspired by the old Roman conception of *Jus Naturæ*, declared that there is a Law of Nature, a beneficial code which has been established by Nature herself, and this furnishes mankind with the standard to which all human policies ought to conform. The sound conclusions of Petty and North as time went on became embroidered with a great amount of fancy work. The swing of the pendulum, so far as these theorists were concerned, was complete. Undoubtedly, many of their doctrines were largely a product of the time. The unfortunate state of affairs existing in France during the latter half of the eighteenth century, lent colour to somewhat fantastic speculations which contained both a political and an economic theory. On the subject of labour, they held that only labour employed in agriculture or the extractive industries is productive. Thus labour employed in manufactures or transport was classed as unproductive, together with that of the professional man and the merchant. To judge of the annual increase of national wealth, it was held by them to be but necessary to calculate the value of the products of field, forest, water, and mine, and deduct the cost of their production. This gives the *produit net*, and is the sole measure of the increase of national wealth. It was indeed conceded by them that manufactures, commerce, and the liberal professions may be useful, but they are unproductive and sterile, drawing their gains from the superfluous products of agriculture, and the number of people employed in them should therefore be reduced to a minimum. These teachings were a necessary protest against the worst fallacies of the Mercantilists. Indeed, in spite of anomalies, the world to-day owes much to the Physiocrats. They had appeared upon the scene at a time when highly artificial regulations were threatening to strangle both commerce and industry. This was the more important, since owing to discovery and invention, trade and business were ripe for considerable expansion. The Physiocrats had a favourite motto, *Laissez faire, laissez passer*, by which they meant, keep your hands off and allow trade to develop along its own lines. Absolute freedom of trade was held to be the surest way to progress, both national and world-wide. For by freeing trade from all possible restrictions, the smallest possible deduction for commercial services would be made from the *produit net* ;—customs-duties, octroi, expenses of Government, and other restrictive regulations, all

in the end caused leakages from the one great fund.
The great interest of the Physiocrat position now is
that the best elements of the system were absorbed by
a very remarkable man, and were by him transmuted
into pure metal. Adam Smith had early in life
set himself a great task—the revision of the whole
range of philosophy. He did not succeed in accomplishing all that he had planned, but after a long
sojourn in France, during which he discussed economic
theories with the leading Physiocrats, he set to
work to produce a great work on wealth and its
phenomena. In the year 1776, he published " An
Enquiry into the Nature and Causes of the Wealth
of Nations." This was speedily recognised as one
of the most remarkable books ever written, and
Adam Smith was acclaimed as the founder of a new
Science. The moment when this book appeared is
marked by some momentous events as one of the
great epoch-making periods in history. For that
same year the American Colonies declared their
Independence and Democracy was born ; and only
a few months earlier James Watt had perfected
his steam engine, which was destined to effect so
many changes in industries and manufactures, and
bring about that great social event known as the
Industrial Revolution.

It is not too much to say that Adam Smith's
book had as powerful an effect on modernising trade

and industry as the steam engine, for it showed the necessity for adopting a different attitude to economic questions, and became the inspiration of a series of statesmen from Pitt to Gladstone, who by their policy smoothed the way and made progress possible. Indeed, but for this new spirit infused into the statesman and legislator by Adam Smith, the new developments would have been sorely hampered.

The theories of Political Economy had been made concrete and simplified by Adam Smith, but the subject was neither limited nor completed by the *Wealth of Nations*. Other thinkers published their conclusions. Ricardo, indeed, was ambitious of rewriting the *Wealth of Nations*. He succeeded in opening up new avenues for speculation by constructing an *economic man*—a useful hypothesis, and a necessary step in the development of the subject. This *economic man*, however, has been the cause of a great deal of misconception and mistrust.

Malthus, too, writing at the time when causes and effects in the industrial world were difficult to determine with certainty, by taking a too restricted view of the situation, and by keeping his attention closely fixed upon contemporary hardships, evolved his law of population and laid the foundations of a theory of wages. This, with Ricardo's theory, gained for Political Economy the title of the *dismal science*.

It is unnecessary here to go in detail into either the theories or the errors of these and other early economic writers. The important point is to realise that an entirely new economic situation had arisen owing to the application of steam power to manufactures. A new set of problems the like of which mankind had never previously faced, yet vitally affecting the well-being and the future of the nation, presented themselves and demanded immediate attention. Neither statesman nor reformer, employer nor employed, had either a precedent to which to refer, or a standard to which appeal might be made. For some decades there was a period of tragedy caused by the fact that, whether with or without good intentions, people were ignorantly groping in the dark. Experience had to be bought, and in this case it was bought at the cost of much suffering, injury to the race, and even death. Unhappily many of the worst sufferers were helpless little children, and women. This forms the darkest chapter in industrial history, and usually its causes and the lessons which may be learned from them are ignored. It is of the utmost moment to those who desire to know the truth about present social conditions to study very carefully the period of the early days of industrialism, for unless this be done, misconceptions will be unavoidable.

CHAPTER III

THE ORIGIN AND DEVELOPMENT OF SOCIALISM IN ENGLAND

SOCIALISM is essentially a modern movement. It originated in the developments which took place in connection with the great changes wrought by the Industrial Revolution ; thus to really understand Socialism as preached in England to-day, a knowledge of English industrial history is necessary. The great revolution caused by the application of steam power and labour-saving machinery to manufactures, very completely transformed the conditions and circumstances of living for the great mass of the nation. Up till that time the population of this country had been comparatively small ; but the opening up of new markets, and the extension of the world's trade, coming just at the time when new processes of production made it possible to supply a large and growing demand, caused population to increase by leaps and bounds. Thus began to arise a new social situation ; a small population, for the most part sparsely scattered over the country, gave place to a comparatively large and ever-growing population, not scattered over the country

C

but concentrated in towns. These towns were to a great extent new, having been called into being by the changed industrial conditions. They had neither tradition nor precedent to rely upon. Their growth had been haphazard ; factories and mills surrounded by the dwellings of the workers were irregularly piled together. At first perhaps this had arisen for convenience' sake, but the final result was that most distressful feature of the modern world, the industrial town of the mid-nineteenth century with ill-paved, irregular streets, large numbers of back-to-back houses, producing in due time all those problems —social, municipal, physical and ethical—connected with the slum. In a sentence—in place of a small population living mainly under rural conditions, there arose a dense town population centred in a comparatively few localities.

The Industrial Revolution led to the production of commodities of all kinds in greatly increased quantities. What had been the comforts or even the luxuries of the wealthy now came within reach of those who were comparatively poor ; indeed, one of the great changes effected by the revolution was that henceforward the manufacturer was to fix his attention more and more on the production of those goods which would command the greatest sale. In other words, it was the needs of the masses which were to be catered for rather than, as had hitherto been the rule, the demands of the wealthy. In no instance perhaps is this great change so clearly seen as in the shipping industry. The *Indiaman* of the eighteenth century had brought to England silks, jewels, perfumes and the hundred and one things necessary for the luxurious life. During the nineteenth century shipping became more and more the means of making the conditions of life for the people more comfortable ; the great object of international commerce being to ensure for the masses food-stuffs and clothing, good, plentiful, cheap, and of a standard never before within their reach.

'At the same time, too, economic thought and practice began to take a new direction. Theorists began to consider the newly developing organisation of industry. The master-craftsman had developed into the *capitalist employer*, the journeyman had become *the hand*. These and other novelties had become part and parcel of the new order of society, and after a few decades, it was confidently assumed that the new state of affairs had come to stay. A too restricted view of any situation invariably results in drawing a false conclusion ; it was so in this case. None of the economists, with the possible exception of J. S. Mill, either went behind or questioned *Capitalism*. Nor was it until great abuses in connection with factory and slum had grown into glaring evils that anyone thought, or indeed dared, to question the new economic conditions.

It is at this point that teachings, feeble at first, but growing in strength and volume, began to make their appearance—these teachings are the beginning of modern Socialism. Gradually a school of reformers arose which was anti-capitalistic, advocating sweeping economic reforms, criticising the existing ideas as to private property and competition—this school was Socialist.

It is well worth while pausing for a moment before considering these new theories, to gain some further idea as to how the new social evils had arisen. Is it conceivable that a group of evil-intentioned men devised the factory system, thought out a policy for sweating labour of all descriptions, of buying cheap and selling dear with the deliberate intention of depressing the condition of the worker, and by these means raising themselves to positions of wealth and importance ? Had any group of men been so far-seeing, had they been able to lay plans so far ahead, and with so great a measure of success, one would almost have to confess that they deserved their reward. But this was by no means the case. Throughout the business world, in connection with manufactures, the labour force, markets, and banking, everything was revolutionised. No one knew exactly what was happening—the whole industrial

world, for a considerable time, was blindly groping
in the dark. There was practically no previous
experience to go upon, no precedents whence
guidance might be sought. Take the banking
sphere, for instance. Here at fairly regular intervals for a number of decades, pressures leading
on to crises and even disaster became the rule.
It seemed to be a law of nature that the business
world must pass through a cycle culminating with a
Black Friday. Subsequent history has considerably
modified this view. Want of knowledge and
lack of experience led bankers, when times of difficulty were threatening, to begin calling in their
advances, and to tighten up their purse-strings ;
they must safeguard themselves whatever might
happen to the rest of the community. Thus, just
to mention a few dates in last century, in 1825, 1833,
1845 to 1847, 1856, 1866 there were commercial
crises. Each of these, however, taught a lesson,
from which experience of the greatest moment was
painfully gathered. The banking interest now
knows how to face an incipient crisis, with the result
that for many years past such phenomena have
been robbed of their worst terrors.

Similar lessons, *mutatis mutandis*, have been
learnt, or are being learnt in all spheres of industry
and commerce, with far-reaching results to the community ; but the ardent social reformer is very apt

to ignore these significant facts. It should be noted, too, that both law and custom had evolved to suit other and simpler circumstances ; it took well-nigh half a century to get even the foundations laid of a system of law suitable to these changed conditions.

When one reads history and realises how long it took to evolve a satisfactory system of Parliament or Justice, both of which were beginning to shape themselves in Norman and Plantagenet times, though a really satisfactory system in each case only resulted after 1688, it must be conceded that though there are many anomalies still existing in the industrial sphere, though there is much to be regretted in social conditions, yet if one compares the state of affairs in 1813 with that of 1913 there is much of which to be proud. Many difficult problems have been fathomed, and the capitalist system (to accept a phrase which has become current) has shown a remarkable elasticity, and the capability of progressing on right lines. There has been a very real evolution in the best sense of the word. Moreover, this is in accordance with the best traditions of our race. It is indeed a great and striking fact that in little more than a century we have realised most of the difficulties and problems connected with the vast revolution wrought by the invention of steam—a revolution prolonged by a series of inventions, greater than the whole previous history of man can show. The English race has boldly faced this difficult situation, and on the whole has faced it wisely. A system has been built up containing elements which warrant our facing the future full of hope. A great deal has been successfully accomplished in a comparatively short time, but what is of even greater moment, the system established with so much travail gives promise of accomplishing yet greater things. Evolution, the great secret of English success in so many spheres, is working, and promises to go on working, in this sphere too.

The thought naturally arises, do the critics of our industrial system really grasp the intricacies of the mechanism of modern commerce ?

Modern Socialism, then, may be said to have originated owing to conditions resulting from the Industrial Revolution. The impossibility of foreseeing where certain forces, if left uncontrolled and subject to ignorant chance alone, would lead, brought about a condition of affairs among certain sections of the working classes which can only be called appalling. It should be pointed out that a great deal of the trouble and misery both of the past century, and even of that now existing, has been caused by an ignorance of economic laws ; especially is this the case in relation to population. The law of population as stated by Malthus was perhaps rather too sweeping and definite ; but it should be remembered that he lived at a time when it seemed as though a certain system would be permanent. What he enunciated was in the main true enough ; it was his successors who, developing his theory on wrong lines, preached an impossible doctrine. The law as he stated it was to the effect that population will increase up to the means of subsistence. And he tried to prove that while population can increase in geometrical ratio, the means of subsistence —the food supply—can only increase in arithmetical ratio. This being the case, an equilibrium must be maintained, and this may be done either by natural or by artificial checks ; the best check is to set and maintain a high standard of comfort. Malthus was perhaps rather too definite, but the working of the law can be easily traced in certain sections of the community. The statistics of slum populations show this. Under slum conditions are found the highest birth rates. It is true that the highest death rates are found there too, but the net increase is also greater than in the comparatively well-off classes. The point is of interest because it bears on various questions, such as that of fixing a minimum wage for sweated workers. So long as these people exemplify the law, and, whilst having a very low standard of comfort, tend to increase up to the means of subsistence, the effect of fixing a minimum wage would merely be to intensify the trouble. With this class of people the first requisite is to implant a real desire for a higher standard of living —this once done, a minimum wage would be beneficial ; otherwise its utility must be very doubtful. There must first come the desire for better conditions, then the possibility of enjoying them ; it is to a great extent true to say that the individual makes the slum, *i.e.* the worst side of slum life.

The situation created by the Industrial Revolution would need much time to describe fully, but from one or two extracts from the speeches and writings of the period a sufficiently good impression can be gained. In the year 1840 Lord John Russell informed the House of Commons that the people of the British Isles were in a worse condition than the negroes in the West Indies. Dr Arnold wrote to Thomas Carlyle that the state of society in England was never yet paralleled in history. Richard Cobden during the Anti-Corn Law Campaign was able to tell stories of people reduced to living on stewed nettles and the meat taken from decayed carcases. Emigration on a large scale was going on, and these emigrants left our shores sullen and angry, nursing a feeling of the bitterest hatred against the old country. The mass of the people

began to look on the Reform - Act as a failure.
Nor had efforts to improve industrial conditions,
whether of a peaceable nature or those accompanied
by physical force, resulted in anything satisfactory
to the workers. Commissions were appointed to
examine into the condition of England ; but the
outcome was nil, for their only practical suggestions
were that riot and possible revolt should be subject
to drastic repression. Lord Melbourne denounced
the criminal character of Trade-Unions and seriously
advocated their suppression.

In 1834 there had been a radical revision of the
Poor Law, but so far as the masses could see, the
only tangible result was the cutting off of doles,
and the rigorous enforcement of the *régime* of the
Workhouse. Then came revelations concerning the
factories—the employment during brutally long
hours of women, and even little children, together
with a mass of evidence of a very horrible state of
affairs. Frederick Engels, the co-worker with Karl
Marx, revealed to continental Europe the state of
things existing in England. Great indeed was the
surprise to hear that in the workshop of the world,
where wealth was being accumulated in hitherto
undreamed-of amounts, the conditions of life for the
great mass of the working classes were intolerable
and unspeakable. It is a sad picture to look back
upon, but it is worth doing if only to grasp an idea

of the great change that has come over industrial
life and its conditions.

As the new state of affairs developed, and the
wage-earners grew in number, the divergence between
their interests and some of the doctrines and theories
of the economists became more and more distinct.
Nor was it long before, from amongst the middle
classes, a new type of thought began to make its
appearance. The labouring population was apparently so environed by the new system that self-help
on right lines was not to be expected. In their
efforts to free themselves from the ever-tightening
grip of untrammelled competition, which was now
the accepted policy of those in authority, they began
to adopt measures whose only result could be the
deepening of the misery of their lot. With un-
educated fervour the doctrine of physical force and
revolutionary excess was preached and to some
extent practised. This it was that inspired men
like Robert Owen and Frederick Denison Maurice
in England, St Simon and Fourier in France, in the
face of a misinformed and unsympathetic public
opinion, to take up the cause of the workers. Self-
help being impossible, it behoved those enjoying
superior advantages of wealth and education to
lead and inspire the helpless workers and endeavour
to put their efforts towards the bettering of their
material and social position on sounder economic

and constitutional lines. The masses if saved at all
must be saved by the middle class. This created
an extremely interesting situation, to understand
which, a sketch of the careers of these self-appointed
leaders is necessary.

Robert Owen was born of comparatively poor
parents at Newtown, Montgomery, in the year 1771.
From his earliest years it was evident that his was
no ordinary personality. Before he was seven years
old he had absorbed all the knowledge that the local
schoolmaster could provide, and himself acted as
teacher in the school. At the age of nine he left
school and spent a year in London; thence he
joined a draper at Stamford, named M'Guffog,
and with him thoroughly learned to judge woven
materials, a knowledge which was to stand him in
good stead during his business life. Before leaving
home some well-intentioned religious ladies had
lent Owen some books on religion. These books,
unfortunately, were not really religious, but were
concerned with religious disputes. The reading of
them had a disastrous effect, for the young boy
began to distrust Christianity which, while professing
to be a religion of peace and goodwill, could lead
to such dissensions. Unhappily, too, Mr M'Guffog
and his wife had disputations on religious doctrines,
and these decided Owen finally to break away from
accepted traditions. It was undoubtedly a great

misfortune, because from what one can gather of
Owen's character, there were all the possibilities of
a strongly religious man there. From Stamford,
Owen returned to London to get further experience
in the drapery trade, and about the year 1788 he
went to Manchester. He arrived in the great textile
town at the psychological moment. After a short
experience of working on his own account, at the
age of nineteen he applied for the post of manager
at a mill employing five hundred hands. He was
the youngest applicant for the position and asked
for the biggest salary, but so impressed was Mr
Drinkwater, the owner of the mill, with Owen's
personality, that he was appointed. With this
managership came out for the first time the rule
that was to be the guiding principle of Owen's life.
All the mills were being equipped with the newly-
invented machinery, and of this the mill-owners
took the greatest care. But between them and
their workpeople the sole bond was what Carlyle
has tersely described as the " *cash nexus*." So long
as the agreed wage was paid, there all responsibility
ceased. Owen at once declared that his policy
would be to take as great care of the living machinery
as of the inanimate. His management was extra-
ordinarily successful, and Mr Drinkwater before the
end of the first year had decided to take him into
partnership at the end of three years. There was

some opposition to this from Mr Drinkwater's son-in-law, and Owen at once severed his connection with the firm. He had no difficulty in finding a niche. His ability was now well known, and he prepared to start in business on his own account in partnership with some Manchester friends. In order to equip the Chorlton Twist Mill with new and up-to-date machinery Owen had to visit Glasgow, and there met his fate in the person of Miss Dale, daughter of the proprietor of the New Lanark Mills. In order to get an introduction to Mr Dale, Owen offered to buy his mills, and succeeded both in doing so and in marrying Miss Dale. For some four and twenty years from January the 1st, 1800, Owen's chief interest was at New Lanark. Here he developed his theory and practice as to the right relations which should exist between employer and employed. The Scot workpeople were at first very suspicious of the strange Welshman, but eventually Owen completely won their confidence. In the year 1812, during a shortage of cotton, many mills, New Lanark amongst others, had to close down for some weeks. No work, no pay, was the general rule. Not so, however, with Owen. Throughout the weeks when the works were closed down, Owen's operatives regularly received full pay, at a cost of something like £7000 ! In another direction, too, Owen wrought a great improvement in the conditions of living for his

workpeople. He found that they were victims of
the small shop, that credit and an inferior quality of
goods cost these folk dear, and that the purchasing
power of their wages was seriously diminished.
To remedy this Owen cleared a floor in the mill,
installed a competent salesman, and laid in a stock
of the ordinary goods consumed by workpeople.
He bought the best quality goods in wholesale
quantities, and was able to supply them at prices
very little more than he paid. Here we have the
beginning of distributive co-operation, the model
copied shortly after by the Rochdale Pioneers.
Moreover, Owen began to develop his theories as to
improving the living machinery for his works. He
opened what he called an " Institution for the Formation of Character." Here the children of his workpeople began their life training at the earliest possible
age. Little toddlers of two years old entered this
Institution : the beginning this of the Infant School.
Owen's educational methods are still of value, and
some of them might be copied with advantage. In
spite of his open-handedness—or perhaps in conse-
quence of it—Owen is credited with having netted
no less than £360,000 in a little over twenty years.
He was one of the most successful mill-owners of the
day, and his model establishment, with its arrangements for the betterment of the workers, became
one of the show-places of Europe. During the last

thirty years of his long life—he lived to be nearly eighty-eight—Owen gave himself up to furthering co-operation, and many social-betterment schemes. These latter ended in failure and disappointment, but the great lesson of Owen's life can never be forgotten. He, first, under the new conditions resulting from the Industrial Revolution, realised, taught, and practised the right relation between employer and employed.

The other English name mentioned, that of F. D. Maurice, belongs to a generation later than Owen. Maurice was the son of an Unitarian minister and was born in the year 1805, a couple of months before the victory of Trafalgar impressed the world that England had definitely and successfully adopted a policy of evolution as against one of revolution. Maurice was carefully educated, mainly by his father, and became a scholar in the true sense of the word. Although the family was outwardly harmonious, as a result of religious discussion, a system of written disputation was kept up. These disputes led to important consequences. First Mrs Maurice became a stern Calvinist, firmly believing in a small body of the elect and a great mass of lost, and unfortunately for her own peace of mind she numbered herself among the latter. One daughter became a Baptist, another an Anglican. Thus, as might be expected, at a comparatively early age young

Maurice felt unable to accept his father's religious convictions. However, when he went up to Cambridge at the age of eighteen he was still a Non-conformist. His career at the University was distinguished, and he might have taken a brilliant degree, followed by a Fellowship of his College, but he shrank from signing the Thirty-nine Articles apparently to ensure self-advancement, so went down without taking his degree. For some time he worked as a journalist with John Sterling in London. Then, finally, deciding to join the English Church, although now twenty-five years old, he entered Exeter College, Oxford, and again worked for a degree. On graduating he also took Orders, and accepted a curacy near Leamington. In the year 1836 he went to London as Chaplain to Guy's Hospital. It is very difficult to picture the state of working-class feeling during those eventful years between 1836 and 1848. As the months passed by a feeling of great uneasiness was experienced all over Europe, and gradually a tide of revolution, surging over the continent, found its way into England. Thrones were tottering, and for a time it seemed as though the Republican form of government would be almost generally adopted. Maurice for one had no doubts as to the best form of government for England. Tense as were his feelings, and deep as were his sympathies with the workers, he

D

mistrusted revolution. Nay more, he had convictions in favour of the monarchy. Nor did he hesitate to voice his views. He boldly declared that although individual kings might be discredited, kingship was not. In State affairs he was a Conservative of the best type. A strong government was the first necessity, but as to how the community living under that strong government should be organised, he took a widely different view from those agreeing with him as to monarchy. It was the duty of the State to safeguard the interests of the individual citizen and protect his property, but what was needed at this time of national crisis was that citizens should work harmoniously together in association, instead of being ranged in two camps separated by a rivalry whose mainspring was cut-throat competition. This attitude was the main plank of the Christian Socialist movement, led by Maurice, Hughes, and Kingsley, and influenced them in both their educational work, which resulted in the foundation of the Working Men's College, and their policy for national well-being, which led them to champion the cause of co-operation.

For a considerable time, however, it looked as though a policy of force would prevail, and the year 1848 in England, as abroad, was a time of tumult. It is unnecessary to repeat the well-known story. London was spared the sight of riot and bloodshed.

Great preparations on both sides were made for the presentation of the monster petition to Parliament, on April the tenth. A large force of special constables, amongst whom was Maurice, was sworn in to keep the peace. The day, like so many in England, was dismally wet, the Chartists' riot fizzled out, and the petition went quietly to Westminster in a cab. Failure for revolution—true; but on that same day Maurice, Kingsley and a few kindred spirits met, and as a result of that meeting the Christian Socialists concreted their organisation, and began definitely to make their views known publicly. Next day London was placarded with addresses to the Working Men of England, telling them that they had friends, unknown personally, it was true, but "who love you because you are their brothers, who fear God and therefore dare not neglect you, His children." These placards were followed by the publication of a small periodical called *Politics for the People*, sold at one penny a number. This little paper had a circulation of about two thousand copies, and although only seventeen parts were issued, the theories and feelings of the editors were strongly and effectively voiced. Maurice began strongly to denounce the selfishness and cruelty of unrestricted competition in industries. "Competition," he declared, "is put forth as a law of the Universe. That is a lie. . . . The payment of wages under this competitive system has ceased to be a righteous mode of expressing the true relation between employer and employed. . . . It is no old condition we are contending with, but an accursed new one, the product of a hateful, devilish theory which must be fought with to the death." It can easily be imagined the outcry that such a declaration caused in certain quarters. But Maurice held on his course ; he was no idle declaimer, nor did he advocate an impossible utopia. His watchword was " association "—a policy based on association would bring hope and salvation to the workers, not only so far as material well-being was concerned, but intellectually and educationally it would be the safest and surest road to the highest culture.

It must, however, be carefully noted that these associations advocated by Maurice were not to be organised and nursed by the State. The workers were called upon to organise themselves, to take their fate boldly in both their hands and go forward. It was the function of the State to see that they had fair play, and to prevent abuses. The Co-operative Producing Associations brought into being by the mutual working and class sympathy of the workers themselves would, if successful, result in the elimination of the excessive profits of dead capital, and the ferocity of the competitive struggle would be lessened. Maurice's dream was that from small beginnings the Associations both for the production and distribution of goods, and the education of the masses, might become universal.

It was thus that modern socialism commenced in England, under leaders like Robert Owen, one of the most successful business men of his time, and Frederick Denison Maurice, a clergyman of the English Church, holding strong views as to monarchy, but advocating associations among working people for both their intellectual and material well-being. It is true that these two men did not see eye to eye on many subjects, especially on religion; but, under somewhat different forms, they preached and practised a very similar doctrine.

CHAPTER IV

WHILST events were occurring in England as just narrated, under different conditions somewhat similar developments were taking place in France. New thoughts by a new school of theorists speculating on economic subjects were destined to have far-reaching results. The criticisms of these men on the situation as it affected the working classes in France, originated in the after-effects of the French Revolution, in combination with the new industrial conditions resulting from the introduction of the factory system. Men like St Simon and Fourier were anti-capitalist—that is to say, they were Socialists ; and, like Owen and Maurice, seeing the want of capability among the masses to create among themselves efficient leaders, saw the necessity for bringing aid to them from members of the superior classes. It was but natural that the wisest and best of the community should endeavour to regenerate society, and this must be done by educating the masses to live under an ideal system. But whilst being socialists they were not revolutionaries, they preached no class warfare. What had to be done was that the masses should be raised, not that those who were better off should be depressed, Here again we have a middle-class movement.

Claude Henri, Comte de St Simon, was born in the year 1760, and claimed descent from Charlemagne. An ambitious man, and withal vain, as may be realised by the order he gave his valet as to awakening him each morning: "Arise, Monsieur le Comte, you have great things to do to-day." He tells how his great ancestor appeared to him in a vision and urged him to devote his life to philosophy, promising him that his successes in that sphere should be as epoch-making as his own had been in arms and statecraft. He was undoubtedly a man of broad views, and held that so far as the present organisation of society was concerned, what was required was amendment, not revolution. As to private property, if it consisted of investments worthy of compensation, it was rightful. As to the relations that should subsist between capital and labour, harmony, not strife, should be the aim—the fight should be between the industrious and the idle. Society ought to be so organised that all its members must work. Indeed, it may be said that one of the greatest, if not the greatest, contribution made by St Simon to the subject was the necessity of work by all. The central teaching of his system was that the labour

of the entire community should be so directed that
the physical and moral condition of all its members
would benefit. To this end the nation should be
organised on an industrial basis. But as the people
were not yet fit to govern in the industrial sphere,
this duty must be entrusted to scientific experts,
industrial chiefs. Government proper would be
limited to other spheres and to giving the heads of
the industrial associations a free hand. Let this
system but once be instituted and " mankind would
cease exploiting one another, and mutually turn
to exploit the earth." Although St Simon did not
actually attack private property, his followers did.
Taking up his teaching as to the necessity for all
to work, they declared that there must be no idle
class ; the idle capitalist living an on unearned
income must have no place in the new society.
Such a man is a parasite, an exploiter of the worker.
Here socialist teaching is becoming very modern.
In criticising the existing system, it was declared
that capitalist employers as owners of the instruments of production are able to dictate their own
terms to the workers. Nor is this all, for, thanks
to the system of inheritance, the instruments of
production are handed on from father to son, even
though the son may be incapable. This too must
be ended, and the community must own all capital.
Here again the teaching is remarkably modern.

François Marie Charles Fourier was born in the year 1772. His father was a prosperous draper at Besançon. By nature young Fourier was a student ; however, bowing to circumstances, he went into business, and once there, worked well and successfully. At a very early age he began giving attention to commercial abuses and the petty tricks of trade. It is related how, as a small boy of five years old, he was severely punished for making some too truthful observation concerning some of his father's stock ! And when a young man of twenty-seven he was roused to anger at having to destroy a quantity of rice which had become unfit for human consumption owing to its having been " held for a rise " during a time when many people were suffering from starvation. His experience led him to the conclusion that the existing system of society was fundamentally wrong, and he set himself to work to think out what the new system should be. Like Robert Owen he advocated a system of association, but his associations must be limited in membership. Eighteen hundred members, he decided, was the ideal number. Such a community could be self-supporting and could reduce the numbers required for protection to a minimum ; thus the great majority would be producers. Much has been borrowed from Fourier by modern socialist writers, *e.g.*—

    " All labour may be pleasant ; it is only overwork that is unpleasant, and that should be unnecessary."

" Change of occupation is good—no man ought to devote long consecutive hours to one piece of work."

" Between the ages of eighteen and eight-and-twenty a man ought to produce sufficient to enable him to live henceforward a life of leisure."

Labour, said he, may be divided into three classes —necessary, useful, and agreeable. Necessary labour deserves the highest reward, but those who choose agreeable tasks deserve the lowest pay. Exertion should be the measure of reward. He also gave currency to the theory of a minimum wage for all. With all his socialism he was not entirely orthodox. There would, he thought, be a surplus after labour had been paid, and he allowed that a third of this surplus should go to capital, thereby showing that he realised the necessity for providing some inducement for thrift. Probably he foresaw that without this reward, capital would not be accumulated.

In the year 1848 the proletarian revolution broke out in France, and after that time the lead in socialist thought was taken by Germany. Socialism ceased to be middle-class. It can hardly be said that there was a definite break ; the early socialism shaded into the modern, and between the two, like a

connecting link, comes Louis Blanc. Born in 1811
at Madrid, the son of King Joseph's Inspector-
General of Finance, Blanc enjoyed the advantage
of a good education and became a tutor and journalist. Turning his attention to writing, he published
a book, *L'Organisation du Travail*, and this made
him very popular with the French working classes.
This book preaches the brotherhood of man and the
need that every individual born into the world
should have the chance to develop his character
and intellect to their fullest capacity. For his work
a man should be paid not according to the quantity
produced, but should receive sufficient for his wants,
that is, he should be able to cultivate any tastes
and talents with which nature had endowed him.
No system should be considered successful unless
every member had his needs supplied. Thus the
great point of Blanc's teaching is the right of every
individual to a chance for fully developing his individuality, and that he shall have the needs of that
individuality supplied. This he considers is not
possible under a competitive régime. He is as fierce
on the subject of competition, as then practised,
as was Maurice. He calls it a murderous warfare.
The plan for his workshops was worked out on these
lines, and as it was clearly impossible that the
workers could establish such workshops themselves,
it was the duty of the State to step in ; but the

State should be limited, so far as management of the workshops was concerned, to appointing the Directors for the first year. Once established, the workers must enjoy the privilege of electing their own Directors. Louis Blanc's originality consists in his having been the first to insist on the necessity of the State taking an active share in the organisation of the work of production. Of his workshops as established in France it is probably true to say that they never had a real trial, perhaps it was not intended that they should ; but under even the most propitious circumstances they must have failed. The dictum that all men should produce according to their faculties, and consume according to their needs, may look well on paper ; but Blanc, like many a social reformer since his time, forgot that very insistent entity—human nature. All men are willing to consume according to their needs, and, when that is the *régime* under which they live, their needs have an insistent way of growing. How many men are willing to work according to their faculties when motive is reduced to a minimum ?

Looking back over the work of these early Socialists, while their theories sound utopian and their writings are tinged with sentimentalism, it cannot be denied that they did influence economics for good both in the theoretical and practical spheres. The whole question of the distribution of wealth, a subject far too scantily treated, was brought into prominence, and its issues were made urgent. They also drew public attention to the possible abuses connected with the institution of private property and the right of inheritance—subjects hitherto unquestioned. In refusing to accept private property as a fixed, unchangeable fact they fell into error. Had they demanded *limitation* in place of *abolition*, they would have been working along sounder lines. Indeed, they would have anticipated the practical policy which has been developing with success in this country since 1894.

Interest in the development of socialist theories during the second half of the nineteenth century shifts over to Germany. Here a school of thought originated and developed, which, although owing much to English and French predecessors, and developing their theories on new lines, turned definitely from the classes to the masses. In a word, socialism became proletarian, and its leaders began to pride themselves on having broken away from the utopian ideals of their neighbours, and on having entered on a path of "Scientific Realism." Foremost, at any rate in point of time, among these new reformers come Rodbertus and Lassalle.

Johann Karl Rodbertus was born in the year 1805, and was the son of a Professor at the University of Greifswald. He studied law at Göttingen and

Berlin, and as a comparatively young man settled quietly on an estate in Pomerania in order to give his attention to economics.   Here he elaborated two main ideas—a labour theory of productivity, and a belief that labour was receiving a decreasing share of what it was producing.   Hence one important part of his work was a criticism of distribution from which he goes on to consider a phenomenon unnoticed before the Industrial Revolution, but now recurring with almost cyclical regularity—commercial crises.

Rodbertus adopts, but exaggerates, a theory originally enunciated by Ricardo as to the part played by labour in production, by declaring that labour produces all wealth ; and he is careful to make his readers understand that by labour he means manual labour only.   He allows that organising ability and brains count for something, but such things are a free gift of nature to the individual possessing them ; this being so the share of production due to them is small, and their reward should not be great.   As to his dictum that the manual labourer who creates all wealth is being cheated out of an increasingly large proportion of what he makes, although there was possibly some colour for such a statement half a century ago, such a position in the light of reliable statistics is no longer tenable.[1]   Rodbertus tells us that there are three

[1] *Cf.* Appendix, *Wages and Prices.*

claimants to the wealth annually produced—the rent of land, the interest of capital, and the wages of labour. Of these the two first exist because labour produces a surplus over and above what is necessary for the subsistence of the worker. The institution of private property places the wealthy in a position of advantage which enables them to seize this surplus for their own use. As a result of this the masses, gaining but a bare subsistence, are unable to develop their higher natures, and this is a great detriment to the well-being of the community. Whether his argument was right or wrong, his conclusion arrested the attention of professed economists, who began to see the necessity for giving very much greater attention to the subject of distribution—*i.e.* the consideration of rent, interest, profits and wages, and especially the two last. That industrialism should result in there being a large class of ill-paid labour, tending to intensify the problems connected with poverty and misery, led him to declare that the economist should no longer be content with ignoring this distressing fact ; and that, if economics is a science, the problem of poverty should be as carefully investigated as the problem of wealth. In theorising on the subject of commercial crises Rodbertus tries to show that with a decreasing wage share the workers' power of purchasing commodities decreases ; thus production tends to become greater than consumption. Manufacturers finding the demand for their goods lessening begin to decrease their output, there is a shrinkage in employment, and the workers are really in the grip of a vicious circle, bad leading to worse.

This may account for bad times and unemployment, but it does not account for recurring good times, and a prosperity which is not confined to one class of the community. If the workers' share was always diminishing, and their purchasing power always decreasing, there would be no recurrence of good times. The theory does not coincide with the facts.

What is his remedy ? He advocates nothing startling or revolutionary. Indeed, he concludes that it will take about five centuries to evolve a system satisfactory to all interests. The poverty of mankind, and the commercial crisis which does so much to intensify it, can only be eliminated by wealth becoming the property of the community. To show how the evolution he hopes for will work, he tells of three great stages in economic development. In the first stage there was slavery, ownership of human beings—that was in the Ancient World. Then comes the stage in which slavery is abolished, but whilst man is nominally free, land and capital are subject to private ownership, the result being that whoever wishes to manufacture goods must

pay rent for the use of land, and interest for the
use of capital—such is the condition of affairs at
the present day.   In the future a new era will appear,
during which land and capital will cease to be subject
to individual ownership ; they will belong to the
user for the benefit of the community.   Rodbertus
calls this the Christian-Social Era.

Realising that benefits coming some centuries
hence have only an academic value to the man in
the street, Rodbertus laid down the lines of a policy
for immediate practice, as calculated to smooth the
way towards better things.   The condition of the
worker should at once be improved by regulation ;
hours should be limited, the amount of work per
man should be regulated, a minimum wage should
be fixed, as also should prices.   Robert Owen in
his Labour Exchanges had made use of a labour
currency, *i.e.* a paper money based not on bullion
but on hours of work.   Rodbertus suggested a
similar expedient, declaring that the adoption of
this policy in its entirety would be calculated to
shorten the time before stage three would dawn.

Ferdinand Lassalle was born twenty years after
Rodbertus, and unfortunately a foolish quarrel led
to a duel which cut short an interesting life at the
age of thirty-nine.   He was the son of a prosperous
merchant, but preferred a University career to going
into his father's business,   He studied philosophy

and philology at the Universities of Berlin and
Breslau, and during his student years he imbibed
democratic republican ideas which as years passed
grew in intensity, and resulted in the foundation of
the Social Democratic Party in Germany.

The English Economists, developing Adam Smith's
teaching on the subject of wages, had built up a
hideous doctrine known as the Iron Law of Wages.
As Lassalle accepted this theory and attacked
capitalism from that standpoint, it is worth while
knowing at any rate a little about it.

Adam Smith in the *Wealth of Nations* points
out that originally the worker received the whole
result of his work ; but as society progressed, rent
emerged in connection with land, and improved
cultivation required increasing amounts of capital.
Hence rent and then interest had to receive a share
of what was produced. The share of the worker
came to be fixed by two things—firstly, the funds
available for his employment, and secondly, the
density of population.   Eventually wages reached a
point at which they sufficed to maintain the population, and were equal to the means of subsistence.
Ricardo followed the same line of thought, but in
place of *means of subsistence* suggested a new phrase,
standard of living. He declared that wages would
conform to the motion which the workers themselves
had formed of the standard of life they would lead,

for that notion would determine the increase of population. Malthus, theorising on the same subject, declared that it was impossible to improve the condition of the poor man by means of money, and so enable him to live better than he did before, without depressing the condition of others in the same class. He thus assumes that a certain fixed amount of the total food produce of a country will go to the working class, and that the total food produce is a fixed amount, so that any increased demand means increase in price, without leading to an increase in supply. These assumptions, it may be noted in passing, may have been true at the time when Malthus wrote, but fortunately those times were exceptional, and so the theory requires modification. However, the subject did not remain undeveloped : both James Mill and his son, John Stuart Mill, carried the theory further ; indeed, the younger Mill gave the final form to the *Iron Law*, which may be briefly summed up as follows :

(i) Industry is limited by capital, but does not always come up to that limit, the increase of capital gives increased employment to labour without assignable bounds.

(ii) It is not all capital which constitutes the wages fund of a country, but only that part of it which is destined for the direct purchase of labour.

(iii) Thus wages depend mainly on the supply and demand of labour, or on the proportion between population and capital. With these limitations of the terms, wages not only depend on the relative amounts of capital and population, but cannot under the rule of competition be affected by anything else. Wages cannot rise but by an increase of the aggregate funds employed in hiring labourers, or a diminution of the number of the competitors for hire.

Here we have a doctrine full of despair for the working classes, for if it were true, efforts successfully made to improve one class of workers would result in depressing some other class. It is hardly to be wondered at that Political Economy was disliked and called the *dismal science*. Happily economists have retraced their steps, and enunciated a far more wholesome doctrine, at once full of hope for the workers, and in consonance with the facts. Wages are not fixed by dividing some definite amount of capital by the number of workers ; the wages fund of a country is only limited by production itself, for wages are paid out of the result of production, and only for convenience' sake out of existing wealth. The working classes then can raise their standard of living, and can demand a greater share of what is produced, without being haunted by the thought that increased wages must necessarily be gained at the expense of their fellows : production itself is the limit, so that a well-organised labour force, with adequate economic knowledge at its command, can successfully take measures to improve the condition of labour as a whole.

This digression was necessary in order to make clear, however sketchily, a very important point. Returning now to Lassalle, he accepted the Wages Fund theory in all its brutality, and declared that such being the position under the capitalist régime, labour is in a hopeless position. The obvious, and only remedy, said he, is to abolish capitalism and reorganise society on a basis of co-operative association, with the State to supply the necessary credit.

Lassalle makes a critical analysis of capitalism and sums up its essentials. First comes division of labour, then production is organised to cater for a world market, thirdly competition is the main motive force, then one favoured class, the capitalists, own the instruments of production by means of which they exploit the wage-earner to whom they pay as wages a bare subsistence and retain a large surplus for themselves. Thus a dead instrument has depressed the condition of the living agent.

In formulating the new doctrine of *conjunctur*, Lassalle attacked industrialism from a new standpoint. There are a series of circumstances or conditions that may favour the fortunate individual, nor are these due to any effort on his part. Nationality, birth, fortunate circumstances generally, bring fortune to certain individuals, whilst others through no fault of their own experience the reverse. Thus to a great extent the individual cannot control his own destiny. Chance in large measure steps in, and this makes it necessary that the control should be in the hands of Society. Moreover, the larger issues, such as wars and crises, are uncontrollable by the individual. Thus the important events which make or mar nations, being not of individual but of social origin, it is for the community to take the lead.

Much of the teaching of Lassalle is so full of interesting surprises that his early death is a cause of great regret. Had he lived to work out his theories more fully and revise them in the light of a ripe experience, there might have been a rich mine of thought, useful to the social reformer and the economist, and perhaps of benefit to the whole community.

CHAPTER V

SOCIALISM had developed considerably between the days of Robert Owen and Lassalle. Self-dependent associations of working men, organised in a free State, unassisted by the State, but working under a system of law giving them free play, had been the dream of the first socialists, then active assistance by the State had been demanded, and this demand had developed into State Socialism. But socialism still remained a matter of association, and it continued to be national. This position, however, was not to be final. The next advance was to be an attempt to make it international and cosmopolitan ; moreover, peaceful methods were to give place to revolution. The new leader, Karl Marx, was a very remarkable man and had a very remarkable history. He was born at Trèves in the year 1818. His father was a lawyer, and hoped that his son would follow in his footsteps. At the Universities of Berlin and Bonn the younger Marx studied law, but, in the process, became interested in history and philosophy. At first he dreamed of an academic career, but in the early forties journalism claimed

71

him, and he became Editor of the *Rhenish Gazette*. During this editorship he became aware of certain deficiencies in his intellectual equipment, and so decided to study economics at Paris. He married, and settled in Paris in the year 1843. Owing to his advanced opinions he was expelled from France two years later and went to Brussels. While there he showed his wit and power as a controversialist by attacking Prudhon's *Philosophie de la Misère*, in a book which he entitled *La Misère de la Philosophie*! During this time too he composed a manifesto for the Communist League; and naturally during the 1848 period he was very busy. In the year 1849 he settled in London, and it was in London that he died in the year 1883. A man of great industry, he worked untiringly in the Library at the British Museum, where he acquired what was probably an unique knowledge of the literature of Economics, and of the history and development of modern Europe. In the year 1864, as a result of the Industrial Exhibition held two years earlier, the International Working Men's Association was founded. There had been a previous attempt at the same sort of thing, which had under the influence of Marx developed into the Communist League. The new association was originally intended to be a means for furthering the genuine interests of the workers of all countries. It was, however, captured by the Socialists, who, finding themselves strong enough, quarrelled with a group of members who were tinged with anarchist proclivities. These anarchists were expelled from the *International*, and the Socialists hoped that they would be able under the leadership of Marx to advance their policy and influence unimpeded. However, after the failure of the Commune in Paris in the year 1871, the *International* languished and died. The final policy of the *International* is interesting, as it was the policy of Marx. This policy was outlined in the most important congress of the association, held at Brussels in the year 1868. There it was declared that mines, land, and the means of communication ought to be the property of the State, which would hand them over to associations of working men to be worked for the common good ; further, that through co-operative societies and the organisation of mutual credit alone could the workers own the instruments of production ; that labour produced all wealth, and therefore ought to enjoy its full reward without any reduction for rent, interest, or profit. It is perhaps only fair to add that at a congress held at Basle a year later, a proposition condemning the right of inheritance was defeated.

In the year 1864, on the death of Lassalle, Marx had obtained control of the Social Democratic movement in Germany, and had redoubled his efforts at agitation. His influence with the dissatisfied elements of labour throughout the world was immense, and probably is greater now than ever it was in his lifetime, although some of his doctrines have lost somewhat of their original force. His great work, *Das Kapital*, has been called the Socialist's Bible, whilst recently the Syndicalists would appear to have drawn a good deal of inspiration from his teachings.

Under Marx, from an ethical point of view, Socialism degenerated, becoming a pure materialism. One authority has said of it : " In passing into its latest or German stage, Socialism gained intellectually, but lost morally."

With a cynicism that was characteristic, Marx accepted and developed what is known as the Economic explanation of history. This theory contains some truth undoubtedly, and is of considerable interest ; it may indeed in some cases serve as a useful antidote to the chivalry, blood and glory school of historical writing ; but extremists have carried it so far that it would, if accepted, deprive history not only of all romance but of all nobleness. Every movement towards truth and right, every attempt to withstand oppression or succour the weak, would be attributed to motives of self-interest. Pounds, shillings and pence would be looked for as the basis of the motive force impelling men along the road of progress. Extremists go so far as to

declare that Mahomet did not win converts so
much by his religious zeal or even military prowess,
but because at a time when it became possible to
develop trade, and the Christian Church held that
trade would lead to fraud, the Koran taught that
trade is approved by Allah, and the faithful may,
without any spiritual disadvantage, take part in
commerce. Or again, the Crusades were not fought
really to re-take the Holy Places from the Saracen,
but because the road-ends at the Levant by which
the merchandise of the East entered Europe were in
the hands of the infidel, who thereby made a huge
profit at the expense of the European consumer.
Even the Reformation is not so much a religious
movement as one which under the cloak of religion
was really organised by the shopkeeping nations to
enable them to break away from the economic
restrictions of the Canon Law. Such interpretations
make human history a poor thing ; all nobleness, all
self-sacrifice, all the higher motives of life are sacri-
ficed to an all-consuming desire for the questionable
advantages of an increasing material wealth. The
earlier Socialists had held that man is innately good,
that amid much that may be regretted there is a real
nobleness to which appeal can be made. Marx
and his school deny this, declaring that all great
changes can be traced to methods of production and
exchange ; that purely material forces dominate

and determine the acts of communities and the social arrangements of nations. Applying such arguments to modern life, Marx has little difficulty in deciding that the worker is at the mercy of the wealthy, that capital exploits labour and makes unjust profits thereby.

As to Marx's economic doctrines it is of interest to examine what he has to say on the subject of Capital, Value, and Surplus Value : on all these his views are incomplete, not to say unsound. His main error consists in ignoring some of the main factors of the economic position.

As to Capital, he tells us that "Money, the final product of the circulation of commodities, is the first form of Capital." Is he juggling with terms or is he ignorant of the elements of Economics ? Economics was a subject with a well-defined vocabulary before Marx began to speculate ; and in using economic terms he should have used them in the ordinarily accepted sense. The Economist in defining Capital teaches that Capital is wealth used in production. This definition tells us at once that there must have been Capital in the world long before money was employed. The first implement that man devised to help him to work to better advantage was the origin of Capital. Capital can exist apart from money, although under modern conditions for convenience sake Capital is mostly spoken of in terms of money. Capital, which to Marx is a vampire sucking the blood of labour, is really the factor in production to which we owe the possibility of relieving work of the greater part of its hardships. Capital viewed aright is the friend which has eased the burden of mankind and made life more bearable. It is capital that brings an eight-hour day within the bounds of practical politics. Marx's error is that he fails to differentiate between the right use and the abuse of a great instrument. A poison abused by an ignorant or wicked person may cause agony and death. The very same poison used by a skilful doctor may not only relieve pain but be a great blessing. To condemn capital wholesale, because in some instances through ignorance or through wrong-doing it may have caused hardship and misery, is to ignore the broad lessons of history.

Moreover, not only does Marx fail to understand what capital is, and ignore its true function, he also fails to realise the importance of the user of capital, and the fact that the use of capital is not restricted to any one man or one class. In all this he continues to mislead the present-day Socialist. The working-man agitator talks airily about taking over the instruments of production ; the Syndicalist urges each group of workers to take possession of the industry with which it is connected and retain the whole product for itself. Everything that is produced is said to be the work of the manual worker : the organiser is a parasite who sucks the life-blood of the worker. For this is the conception of the position, and is the explanation of the class war that is so recklessly preached.

Really capital is an instrument in production, and in common with all instruments must have a user. It cannot set itself in motion. There is, moreover, a great danger connected with capital. It owes its existence to thrift and abstinence (it is a common socialist gibe to retort " the abstinence of the millionaire ! ")—without thrift and abstinence this instrument would never have existed. When a man makes use of capital in business he runs a great risk, because capital can only be used by consuming it. Thus, unless the user produces, firstly, an equal amount to replace what he has destroyed, and then a further quantity to pay the lender for his thrift, and himself for his risk, the community suffers because the capital available for industry has been decreased in amount. As a matter of fact the man who can successfully make use of capital is skilful above the average. The brain power may or may not be of a very high order, but it is comparatively rare. Many people can be trained to use successfully the ordinary tools and instruments of daily life, and even though they be bunglers the instruments are not necessarily destroyed; they can generally be used again. But Capital once used is lost, and must be replaced—a miscalculation, an error in judgment, a want of skill on the part of the user, and the Capital utilised, having been consumed in the using, is lost. This is the explanation of high profits for successful business men, high salaries for skilful organisers—a fact conveniently ignored by Marx and his followers.[1] High profits and high salaries are not necessarily made at the expense of the wage-earner; indeed, in many instances, as is well known, it is by the best organised business firms, making the best profits, that the highest wages are paid and the most regular employment is given. Not only do these theorisers ignore the importance of the "Captain of Industry," but they ignore the fact that the use of capital is not restricted to one favoured class of the community.

The Capitalist Class, to accept the Socialist expression, enjoys no law of entail. Compare the history of commercial families with that of those connected with land. The general experience in business is that a firm, on the average, ceases to exist with the third generation. Our industrial history, since the introduction of steam, tells with almost wearying repetition of the appearance and success of the self-made man. The explanation is

[1] *Cf.* Appendix, p. 135.

that the ability to organise work and use capital to advantage is no hereditary characteristic.   And in a country like England, ability, like murder, " will out."   Let a man but once show his integrity, and his ability to organise, and he has but little difficulty to find supporters.   It may be difficult to make the initial advance, but the man of grit is not deterred by difficulties, as is proved by the biographies of our leading manufacturers and commercial men.

Not only, however, does one find Marx to be unsatisfactory in his teaching on the subject of Capital and the Capitalist, but he is equally unsound when he treats of Value.   He tells us that " Leaving out of consideration the utilities of commodities, they have all one common property.   They are all the product of human labour ; not of any particular kind of human labour, but of human labour in the abstract.   The value of a commodity is the amount of abstract human labour embodied in it."   And he adds that the more value there is in a commodity the more labour there is embodied in it.   In other words, the cause and basis of value is labour. Although there is a partial truth here, it is stated absolutely, without modification, and as stated the theory will not bear criticism.   The Economist says that value is caused by utility together with limitation in quantity.   That is to say, that where a commodity is useful and to the extent that its quantity is limited, it will have value. This definition will bear all tests. The theory that value is caused by labour will not. For instance, a man picks up a nugget of gold weighing half a pound. Is the labour entailed in stooping down and picking up that nugget worth about twenty-three pounds ? And yet that is what the fortunate finder will be able to sell the nugget for. Again, if labour is the cause of value, when a commodity has once been made its value will not be subject to alteration. A man makes a chair, and, when finished, the chair is worth, say, two pounds. If the labour embodied in that chair is really the cause of its value, the chair will always be worth the two pounds, no more and no less, because you cannot add to or take from the labour which has been expended. And yet furniture emporiums have "sales at great reductions " ! To show the absurdity of the theory it has been wittily asked, " If labour is the sole cause of value, what is the cause of the value of labour itself ? " The theory will not bear criticism.

It is, however, on the subject of surplus value— the great contribution made by Marx to economic thought—that the greatest fallacies concerning the relation between capital and labour have been built up. According to this theory, the capitalist buys from the worker the *use value* of a day's labour for its exchange value or cost. The difference between

F

these two is the *surplus value* which the wicked
capitalist retains, and by means of which he waxes
fat. A popular explanation of this theory is given
in a little pamphlet written by Mr J. Bruce
Glasier, entitled, *How Millionaires are Made*. This
pamphlet, price one penny, is to be found on sale
at most socialist meetings and bookstalls. The
story embodies the working of the *surplus value
theory*. The story is interesting because it not only
contains the theory but its refutation ! It is worth
while, therefore, giving the story in outline. John
and James were two brothers. They had been well
brought up, and then put to the engineering trade,
one as a blacksmith, the other as a turner and
fitter. Both were intelligent, but neither showed
any symptoms of unusual ability or genius. They
worked fairly hard, and *had been* honest, and ex-
ceedingly thrifty. But they did not grow rich.
Their wages were thirty shillings a week, and it was
only by exercising the greatest care that they could
save five shillings a week. To become millionaires
at this rate they calculated would require 80,000
years, and yet some men had made several millions
in a dozen years or so ! It could not be by saving
that working men became millionaires. They
continued their calculations, and found that, at
thirty shillings a week, a working man in thirty
years, that is rather longer than the ordinary working

life, would only receive £2340—very far short of a million. The question was for a long time considered by these young men, and at length light dawned. " No man ever became rich in this world so long as he was content to be a working man merely." He must get hold of other men's labour, become an employer, a capitalist, if he wishes to become rich. If anyone wishes to be a rich man he must hasten out of the " position of being a mere honest workman, as he would hasten out of a house infected with cholera or smallpox." Then John and James decided to become rich if they could. Their savings had mounted up to twenty pounds each. Just as they came to this decision there was a great demand in their neighbourhood for iron construction work. The brothers therefore rented a shed and got in some simple tools and fittings by a wise expenditure of their forty pounds. They then approached one of the contractors who was very busy, and offered to do some part of his contract at a cheap rate if he would supply the materials. The bargain was struck, the brothers left their old employment and started in business. They worked hard, and they worked long hours, and now they found that, as their own masters, the longer and harder they worked the more money they made. A month finished their first contract, and they found that after allowing for all outlay on material, wear and tear of tools and rent, they had cleared fifty shillings a week as wages. Or if they allowed ten shillings each for overtime, they had made a profit off their own labour of ten shillings a week each. The brilliant idea then occurred to them, If we can make ten shillings a week profit on our own labour, why not make it on the labour of other men too! They therefore arranged to take a larger contract, and per-suaded several of their former fellow-workers to work for them. On the completion of the contract their expectations were fulfilled; they had made a profit of ten shillings a week on each man employed. They rubbed their hands gleefully. . . . " We have found the way at last."

The story continues until both brothers had prospered and become wealthy men. One got into Parliament, and so on. The whole thing accom-plished by exploiting labour, by taking possession of the surplus value created by the worker. Is this the real or only explanation? Surely not: the whole explanation is forced and coloured to suit the doctrine. The story is true enough, and can be easily duplicated many times over by turning to the history of our successful manufacturers. What are the real causes of the success of John and James?

The story tells us that neither of these men showed any symptoms of unusual ability or genius; but surely as their little history unfolds itself this

statement is contradicted. They begin by thinking
out how people become rich ; they exercise thrift
and save twenty pounds each ; they seize the
psychological moment for making use of their savings ; they note the effects of their first attempt
at contract work and lay plans for extending their
business. Just these few points show that John
and James were not merely ordinary working folk.
They were far-seeing, capable young fellows upon
whom the experience of daily life was not thrown
away. But their success was due to something
more than their own labour. The Economist tells
us that the origin of capital is abstinence and
thrift, and here we see this dictum exemplified in a
very practical way. The Economist also tells us
that there are three factors in production—namely,
land, labour, and capital. Here again we have an
illuminating illustration of the truth of their asser-
tion. John and James by thrift save a little capital
of forty pounds ; by means of this they rent a piece
of land with a shed on it ; on the land they employ
first of all their own labour, and when they begin
to prosper they employ other men's labour. Could
one wish for a better illustration of the truth of the
teachings of economics ? In a sentence, the experience of John and James has been and will be the
experience of many a steady, industrious man who
has practised thrift and has a genius for organisation.

Without their capital, and without their organising power, these young fellows would have accomplished nothing out of the ordinary. With organising capacity alone they might have been able to show their ability to organise a business successfully, and then to have borrowed sufficient capital with which to start in business. The theory of surplus value as made use of by Marx and his followers is sheer moonshine. What Marx calls surplus value is the wages of the skilful business man ; as there are grades in the skilfulness of labour, or in the fertility of land, so there are grades in the skill of the men who lead the business world ; and the most skilful organiser can make the greatest profits, or can earn the highest salary, if he accepts a position as manager to a company or a trust. Socialists will never carry on practical business concerns if they continue to ignore the importance of the functions of the organiser of industry and his worth to the community. Thus one finds that Karl Marx when theorising on capital, value, and surplus value is unsound ; yet it is on these foundations that he builds up his indictment against the existing organisation of industry, which he calls capitalism. No one is infallible, and there is of course the possibility that Marx's judgments may be correct, but is it thinkable that a sound conclusion can be drawn from such unsound premisses ?

CHAPTER VI

HAVING now outlined the origin and development of Socialism down to the time of Karl Marx, the question arises, what is Socialism to-day ? what are its present aims and teachings ? To answer this question adequately would require a good deal of space, but an examination of some of the literature circulated by Socialists among the working classes in this country is at the present time of considerable interest. Thus, having collected a number of these booklets and pamphlets, I propose to quote and criticise some of their doctrines and statements.

One pamphlet written by Mr Robert Blatchford is entitled *What is this Socialism ?* At the beginning the author explains that " this is not a defence of Socialism : it is an explanation of Socialism. There is not room in this pamphlet to prove that Socialism is just and practical and desirable. The object here is to explain what Socialism is—and is not. A great deal of the hostility to Socialism arises from misunderstanding as to what Socialism is. This misunderstanding is due to the misrepresentation of Socialism by its opponents." Mr

Blatchford then proceeds to say what Socialism is not. "Socialism is not a scheme for seizing the property of the rich, and sharing it out among the poor. Plans for a national 'dividing up' are not Socialism : they are nonsense. 'Dividing up' means individual ownership: Socialism means collective ownership." Then having explained how the people of Manchester own their tramway system, he continues, "To 'divide up' the tramway system would be anti-Socialism. Socialism is the opposite of 'dividing up.' Socialism is collective ownership. That the people of England should collectively own England and all that is in England, as the citizens of Manchester own the trams ; that is Socialism." And again, "Socialism is not a plan to despoil the rich : it is a plan to stop the rich from despoiling the poor. Socialism is not a thief ; it is a policeman."

In the next section Mr Blatchford deals with "*What Socialism Is.*" "Socialism is a system of national co-operation. It is based upon the principle of co-operation as opposed to the principle of competition. It is based upon the principle of collectivism as opposed to the principle of individualism. It is union as against disunion, order as against anarchy. It means each for all and all for each, as against the present cruel and wasteful system of 'Every man for himself and the devil take the hindmost.'" He goes on to quote some definitions of Socialism from dictionaries and the *Encyclopedia Britannica*, and tells us that three of the most popular . . . English books on Socialism are, *The Fabian Essays*, *Merrie England*, and *Britain for the British*. He quotes from the *Fabian Essays*, " Socialism is the common holding of the means of production and exchange, and the holding of them for the equal benefit of all."

Merrie England says :

" Socialists do not propose by a single Act of Parliament nor by a sudden revolution to put all men on an equality and compel them to remain so. Socialism is not a wild dream of a happy land, where the apples will drop off the trees into our open mouths, the fish come out of the rivers and fry themselves for dinner, and the looms turn out ready-made suits of velvet with gold buttons without the trouble of coaling the engine. Neither is it a dream of a nation of stained glass angels, who always love their neighbour better than themselves, and who never need to work unless they wish.

" Socialism is a scientific scheme of national organisation, entirely wise, just, practical. It is a kind of national co-operation. Its programme consists, essentially, of one demand, that the land and all other instruments of production and exchange shall be the common property of the nation, and shall be used and managed by the nation for the nation."

Britain for the British says :

" Here in plain words is the *principle* or root idea on which all Socialists agree :

" That the country and all the machinery of production in the country shall belong to the whole people (the nation) and shall be used *by* the people *for* the people. This · is the principle of collective or national ownership, and co-operation or national use or control.

" Socialism may be summed up in one line, in four words, as really meaning ' Britain for the British.' "

A page further on Mr Blatchford continues : " Under Socialism all the work of the nation would be organised . . . so that no one need be out of work, and so that no useless work need be done. . . . At present the work is not organised, except in the Post Office and in the various works of the Corporations." This travesty of facts requires no criticism. Later on we read : " We have in England thousands of acres of good land lying idle because it does not *pay* to till it ; and at the same time we have thousands of labourers out of work who would be only too glad to till it." How many of our unemployed could make a living out of even our most fertile land ?   It would be cruel kindness to transport starving dock labourers and mock them by saying, " There is the land, make your living out of it." To cultivate the land requires training and knowledge.

To read Mr Blatchford one would imagine that the kindly ground merely needs to be scratched by a man, be he never so ignorant, and food will at once appear.

Can you argue that because the Government [1] is responsible for the Post Office, and because some municipalities have their own gas, water and electric lighting departments, that therefore the community can construct its own ships, make its own clothes, prepare its own food and build its own houses, better under Socialism than is done at present ? Government and municipal enterprise at present has the tax-payer and the rate-payer behind it. When this source of credit and revenue has disappeared how are all these enterprises to be financed ? But as to this more anon.

Towards the end of the pamphlet Mr Blatchford assures the reader that " Socialism would begin by making sure that there should not be a single untaught, unloved, hungry child in the kingdom ; that there should be no such thing as poverty, lack of employment, ignorance, preventable disease, starvation and despair, within the borders of the British Islands. Socialism would provide work, education, food, clothing, shelter, clean and pure air and water

---

[1] The present unrest in the Post Office (1913), and the unjustifiable strike of municipal employees at Leeds, have come as a rude shock to those who believed in State and municipal enterprise as the best means for allaying the unrest in the Labour World.

for all." And a little further on : "Socialism would abolish all that misery, and suffering, and wrong."

Yes ! what a pretty picture have we here of the Earthly Paradise. Could we believe in the possibility of *Socialism* or any other " ism " doing one-tenth part of what is so glowingly painted, one would be willing to sacrifice even life itself to assist in its attainment. Throughout the reading one sympathises deeply with the aim, but sober common-sense tells one that it is easier to say that the State is going to do all these things for the benefit of all, than it is to frame a practical policy for carrying them into effect. In none of these pamphlets is there a satisfactory account of how all is to be accomplished. The question inevitably occurs, here we have writers glibly saying that the State is going to organise and carry on the everyday work of the community—are these men themselves competent to aid in the work ? Could any one of them undertake successfully even the superintendence of one big manufactory or shipbuilding yard ? What system of cost accounting, what methods of store-keeping, what organisation to prevent the thousand and one leakages that can take place in a big manu-facturing business would they adopt ? Organisation does not grow spontaneously. Most of our big firms have been developed from small beginnings, the system has been evolved under careful management.

Yet it is airily declared that the community can do everything for itself, from building a battleship to growing its own food supply, and that apparently without any special knowledge or training for the work.

Another little pamphlet, called *Is Socialism Possible ?* by Mr Eldred Hallas, after treating of such subjects as present conditions, the artisan, the capitalist, State employment and others, asks the question : How can it be done ? After showing what invention has done for modern civilisation, he concludes that the State ownership and control of new inventions is the readiest and fairest way to Socialism. Beginning with that, the next steps are the nationalisation of canals, railways, mines and minerals, then the land ; eventually the State obtains complete ownership. When that has been accomplished, " Each district would have its complement of doctors, nurses, dentists, domestic servants, expert gardeners, window cleaners and other officials who would be in the pay of the State. Until there is universal disarmament England will require to keep a small but efficient standing army, and in addition thereto, at least one half of the adult males should be trained to the science of war. Home Rule should be given to all our possessions beyond the sea as soon as it is believed the people are *strong and wise enough to look after themselves.*[1]

[1] The italics are not in the original.

England by this time would be *producing the bulk of her food supply ; indeed, all her own wheat,*[1] and with no food supply from, or possessions beyond the seas to protect, the navy could be reduced almost to vanishing point. . . . The hitherto wealthy man would be found a position, as far as possible, according to his tastes and capacity, and his increased usefulness would in no way minimise the real pleasures of his life.   Indeed, they would be enhanced by the change.   Travel and every other form of recreation would be possible to all, for every human being would be a member of the aristocracy of the world.   There will be beauty and love and laughter. There will be health and contentment and peace. The shadows of poverty and strife will vanish before the glowing sunlight of the Golden Age, the Socialism of to-morrow."

One rubs one's eyes, one thinks of human nature at its best, and at its worst ; one compares reality with the dream, and wishes that it could be true. The practical question confronts one, How and when is all this to be accomplished ?   Rodbertus did speak of five centuries as being necessary before a much less ambitious dream could be realised. Present-day writers apparently expect the bigger vision to appear within the lifetime of the present generation.   Moreover, all this is to be effected by

[1] The italics are not in the original.

the simple process of the State taking possession
of all the instruments of production and by nation-
alising the land and means of communication.
England is to grow all her foodstuffs, her shipping
is to be scrapped, and yet travel is to be free and
open to all; our colonies and dependencies are to
be cut adrift, willy-nilly, as soon as they are wise
enough to govern themselves ! The idle rich man
is to be given an occupation according to his ability
and is guaranteed happiness ! There appear to be
a good many contradictions, and in giving up so
many of our skilled industries should we not
suffer irreparable loss ? Can we put all our naval
architects and skilled shipbuilders on the land to
grow wheat, and expect them, like the ex-idle rich
man, to be happy ?

Let us try to be serious. The State is going to
take over all existing accumulations of capital—this
is the great secret. But until we alter the present
basis of society this would be a very drastic step, even
though the owners of the capital were compensated.
Moreover, it is necessary to remember what capital
is, and how it functions. Capital is wealth used in
producing more wealth ; it is an instrument, and a
very delicate one, because it is consumed in the using ;
it must be replaced and added to or progress will
cease. No arrangements are made for any of these
contingencies in the proposals of Socialism. The

proposals are kindly and well meant, but utterly impracticable. Moreover, one gets confused, for while some Socialist writers rely upon the State to do everything, others foretell the end of the State! This phase began with Frederick Engels, the co-worker with Marx, but it is also quite modern, for in another booklet, in which is printed a paper entitled " Socialism—a paper read before the Albany Press Club," by Mr W. S. M'Clure, the Socialist Labour Press, while publishing the paper, prefix an explanatory note which is enlightening, not to say amusing.

" On one point the difference is marked and must not be overlooked. Mr M'Clure in several passages seems to suggest that the new society will have its affairs directed by a redeemed State, which, though elected in much the same way as at present, will have been washed in the cleansing waters of the revolution and made whiter than snow. This is not the position of the Socialist Labour Party. It is inconceivable that the State, an engine brought into existence solely for the purpose of maintaining the domination of a ruling class (slave-owning, feudal, or bourgeois) will be either useful or necessary in a society in which classes have ceased to exist. Everything points to the fact that the administration of the material resources of society will be directed, not through elected rulers, but by the workers themselves acting through delegates appointed for the purpose. The Industrial Union, which seeks to unite the workers as a class to do battle against capitalism, will, when capitalism is overthrown, supply an effective mechanism for the direction and control of the new Republic without the need for perpetuating any State Bogey, purified or otherwise."

This prefatory note would appear to be a modified, or perhaps one should say developed, Socialism, a sort of half-way house on the road to Syndicalism.

The present aim of Socialism, from the few quotations given, is to reconstruct society entirely in the interests of all sections of the community. This is a great and worthy aim ; nay more, at a time when so many people are living with no ideal before them, Socialists win our admiration by coming forward with a great ideal. Their criticism of existing conditions, the misery and hopelessness of the submerged tenth, the overlapping of effort, the waste of energy in many directions, the luxury and idleness of a favoured few, these things ought to be made known, and the injury to society proclaimed. That there are abuses, even great ones, in the present system must with shame be admitted, but the socialist critics show no power of discrimination— all the well-to-do are parasites, there is no good to be found in any Captain of Industry, or organiser of business—all the poor are martyrs, all the rich

G

are blood-suckers. The luxury and waste of the middle and upper classes are noted, and one has to confess that such waste does go on. But is waste and extravagance restricted to these classes ? Is it not a fact that it is a failing which pervades every rank in this country ? At a recent meeting where the minimum wage question was discussed, a Socialist pleaded for an increased average wage for every worker of five shillings a week, at a cost of one hundred million pounds a year. In answer to a question he admitted that the annual drink bill of the working classes in this country is just the sum named. No one except a rabid teetotaller would urge that all wage-earners should give up the use of alcohol entirely ; but think for one moment what the real cost of excessive drinking is to the workers. Begin with half or one-third the total outlay, then add lost time on *black* Mondays and Tuesdays, and when to that is added the cost of illness and crime connected with the excess—a really big bill begins to mount up ; and yet that does not sum up the waste and extravagance of the workers. Those who have studied the question declare that the loss in connection with betting and gambling is greater than that connected with drink. One does not wish to imply that the workers should have no recreations, but simply to point out that waste and extravagance are not restricted to the nominally

wealthy. On all hands there is urgent need for
reform, many abuses require checking or removing
altogether. As to this, one is in agreement with the
Socialist ; it is when remedies are proposed that a
divergence of views becomes apparent. We are
asked to go back on all the teachings of history,
and on all our traditions ; the work of those who
built up our position in trade and empire is to stand
condemned. One is asked to agree to a revolutionary reversal of policy and practice. Think for a
moment of the magnitude of the proposal. No
nation has ever cut itself away from its past
without suffering incalculable loss. Consider
secondly what the consequences of even a partial
failure would be—consequences which would be
felt in the first instance, and fall most heavily on
the very classes of the community it is hoped to
raise and benefit. Then pause and decide whether
a policy based on misconception and error is likely
to be successful. So long as the Socialist refuses
to pay attention to natural laws ; so long as he
flouts the real origin, function and use of capital,
whilst he disparages the services of the man who can
successfully organise business enterprise ; so long
as he remains ignorant of the real cause of value, it
must be impossible to accept his theories for social
and national amelioration. The pity of it is that
such earnest men should stultify themselves. For

the workers are showing that they will not be content to remain in ignorance of economic laws and history, nor can there be much doubt but that the hope for the future lies in the effort that the workers are making to get real knowledge. The great root cause of all the difficulties connected with the present situation has been, and is, ignorance. With a right knowledge of economic forces and economic laws, with a wise spirit of compromise rightly used in the interests of all, and with a desire for harmony and not strife, we may expect improvement in the real health and wealth of the community.

Syndicalism

During the past two years a new development in labour organisation and tactics in the United Kingdom has been much discussed. In the April of 1912 an article in *The Times* newspaper said : " The existence of a strong Syndicalist movement can no longer be denied. . . . Its rapid development has taken everyone by surprise, including both the older Trade Unionists . . . and the Socialists who have dominated them. Even careful observers, who have made some study of Syndicalism abroad, were unprepared." Mr Ramsay Macdonald, more recently, in his booklet on Syndicalism, assures us " that all that is happening in England at present is

that Trade Unionism as an active force is reviving
and that industrial action is being resorted to with,
perhaps, the over-enthusiasm which always follows
upon a period of over-neglect." And again, " Syndicalism in England is negligible, both as a school of
thought and as an organisation for action."

In September 1912 the Trade Union Congress
for the first time debated Syndicalism, and its
supporters were hopelessly beaten on a division by
1,693,000 votes to 48,000. Yet that comparatively
meagre number includes some very active, not to say
able, leaders, and it is clearly right to know something about the movement, especially as Dr Arthur
Shadwell tells us that " the efforts made by Labour
politicians and Socialists to prove that it (Syndicalism)
is negligible show that they do not think so. When
men really think a thing negligible they neglect it."

The word Syndicalism is new to the English
language. The ordinary dictionaries do not contain
it, the nearest word—Syndicate—is described as an
association carrying out a financial operation,
which clearly is not an explanation of Syndicalism.
The new word comes from France, and there has a
special meaning, for it denotes the policy of the
Confédération Générale du Travail, whose object is
to destroy, by force if necessary, the existing organisation of industry, and transfer industrial capital
from its present owners to Syndicalists, the Syndical-

ists being the revolutionary Trade Unions. The whole history of the movement in France has been collected by Dr Louis Levine, and has been published by Columbia University under the title of *The Labour Movement in France—A Study in Revolutionary Syndicalism*. Briefly, the object of the Syndicalists is to be accomplished by means of a policy beginning with the irritation strike, to obtain shorter hours and more wages, the employment of *sabotage* (injuring employers by bad work, damage to machinery and so on), leading on to the general strike, as its great and final weapon.

It is possible that the inspiration for such a policy originally came from the secession of the Plebs in Roman history. A century ago Mirabeau spoke of the great power of a united proletariat. But it was not until 1868, at a Labour Congress at Brussels, already referred to as making public the policy of Karl Marx, that it was declared that if production were stopped for a time society could not exist, and it is only necessary for producers to cease from work in order to make government impossible.

To understand the present labour situation it is necessary to have some idea of the relationship between employer and employed during the past century—how that relationship stood, how it has developed, and how it stands now. Although it is impossible to do this fully here, it is possible, by

means of an outline sketch, to make the position
sufficiently clear for the immediate purpose. The
connection between capital and labour at, or just
after, the industrial revolution was tersely described
by Carlyle as a *cash nexus*. A man agreed to work
so many hours a week for so much money. When
the service had been rendered and the money paid
all obligation ceased ; the employer felt no further
responsibility, the conditions of living for the
worker were no concern of his. Under the existing
system of competition he had to buy in the cheapest
market and sell in the dearest ; the cheaper he
purchased the labour necessary for his industry the
better would he be able to compete. Here we have
a simple wage system governed by supply and
demand—but below the surface such a system
entailed, in many instances, much injustice, misery
and suffering. Superficially the worker had the
advantage of being free from all responsibility as
to how the factory should be organised and managed
—he surrendered his share of what was produced
for an agreed wage paid at conveniently short
intervals. But things are seldom so simple as they
appear on the surface. The individual workman
working for his daily bread, with wife and children
depending on his earning power, was in a position
of disadvantage when bargaining with a comparatively wealthy manufacturer. Individual bargaining

placed great power and special advantages in the
hands of the ordinary employer. Hence efforts
were early made to effect a modification of the *cash
nexus* and individual bargaining; this opened a
second chapter in the relations between employer
and employed. Workmen's combinations came into
existence, and with the dawn of collective bargaining,
even though the " Union " was small and its sphere
restricted, labour was more on an equality for
purposes of bargaining with the employer than it
had been : the average employer and the local
Union were very much on a par in this respect.
The conflict of interests emerged in the first period
and continued in the second, the possibility of
friction and class warfare could be foreseen by
those taking far-sighted views. Hence about this
time began attempts to bring about an identification
of interests between employer and employed; this
was the work of Robert Owen and the early Co-
operators. A good system of co-operation would
lead to harmonious working between all the factors
in production. The employers on their side at this
time, partly to wean the men from the Unions and
partly to enlist the interest of the best men in their
work, commenced in a tentative way giving bonuses
for extra work or skill. This marks the beginning
of the bonus system, which has had both good and
bad effects.

A third chapter in the story opens with the application of the Limited Liability principle to business. This gave the employers a new advantage over the men, and was answered by Unions in the same trade associating, and we get Associated Unions such as the A.S.E. These associations might be stronger than the average Limited Company; thus the employers began developing the bonus system with profit-sharing so as to strengthen the identification of interests and weaken the unionist position. So far as co-operation was concerned it was found that it succeeded as a distributing agent, but failed when applied to production. The reason for this was twofold. Co-operators had succeeded in getting legal protection for their organisations, but the Act of Parliament which did this — the Industrial Provident and Partnership Act (1851)—led to the demand for the possibility of the Capitalist trading under limited liability conditions. In essence this is another form of co-operation, but it had the advantage of experience to guide it; for instance, while those responsible for its organisation knew the value of the good manager or organiser, the early co-operators made the fatal mistake of thinking that no man is worth more than about five pounds a week, with the result that the best brains have usually been at the disposal of the capitalist employer. The next stage found the employer

in the stronger position, for Limited Liability trading
was discovered to possess many advantages. To
this the men answered by attempting to federate
their Unions, a policy in which they had considerable success. Then as friction and unrest grew,
conciliation boards for settling wages and conditions
of work were advocated, and collective bargaining
was put on a more satisfactory footing. Profit-
sharing as a harmoniser developed, in some cases,
into a new system called Co-Partnership, and this
was found to work well in cases where employment
was fairly regular, such as gas works, textile and
boot factories. Such industries have worked successfully under this policy, and it has been suggested
as a remedy for railway troubles, and as suitable
for municipal trading departments.

Finally, the latest chapter of Industrial History,
the present time, gives us a situation full at the
same time of great possibilities for good and of
great dangers. Here we have the tendency for all
employers of labour to be ranged together against
an increasingly powerful organisation of all labour,
with the possibility of the sympathetic strike and
the whole programme of syndicalism as the last
word of labour, pitted against a federation of capital
in which the tendency is for all employers to take
their place. Hence a situation full of danger,
full of complications, thanks to the intricate working

of the modern community, but happily full of hope
for the betterment of all. For given wisdom and
moderation, a right statesmanship at the psychological moment, and we may evolve just that policy
which will mean harmony and contentment in the
industrial world, so far as such things are possible
in this imperfect stage of existence. The complexity
of the situation ; the interdependence of the many
factors ; and the realisation that it is the future of
the nation itself which is at stake, has led to Parliamentary interference in trade disputes ; to increased
activity on the part of the Board of Trade ; and
the feverish haste of the Press to make known
every possible view or policy on the labour question.

The simple issue is between class war and industrial
harmony—between continual and wasting friction,
and identification of interests leading to increased
productive power, and a possibly higher standard
of living for the great mass of our population.

With this facing us, it is interesting to know
what Syndicalism, so urgently advocated by some
ardent spirits, means. One writer on the subject
assures us that class war is the basis of Syndicalism ;
if that be so it stands self-condemned. Its advocates
declare that society is divided into two great classes
—the exploiters and the exploited. Syndicalism is
to end this, for under it the workers who produce
all the wealth are to have the full enjoyment of all

that they produce. The State, says the Syndicalist,
even though it became the employer could not effect
this, but it can be done through the Trade Union.
Syndicalists say that the worker cannot be free until
he controls the means of production. In this they
bear company with Socialists, but the two parties
differ in their ultimate object. Socialists wish to
dethrone capitalism, and to organise society on a
new basis, giving to all members of the community
a level chance. This may be utopian, but it is not
anti-social. The policy of socialism contains much
that can be admired by all, and their aim—the
raising of humanity—is one of the grandest possible.
Syndicalists only nominally decry capitalism. Their
real object is to put themselves, or the workers, in
what they consider the favoured position of the
owners of capital. Thus they wish to seize the
whole means of production for the benefit of manual
labour and that only, to the detriment of all other
sections of the community. Mr Tom Mann asks :
" Who is to control industry ? The industrial
syndicalist declares that to run industry through
Parliament, *i.e.* by State machinery, will be even
more mischievous to the working class than the
existing method, for it will assuredly mean that
the capitalist class will, through Government
departments, exercise over the natural forces, and
over the workers, a domination even more rigid

than is the case to-day. And the Syndicalist also
declares that in the near future the industrially
organised workers will themselves undertake the
entire responsibility of running the industries in
the interests of all who work, and are entitled to
enjoy the results of Labour."   If this policy was to
be carried out legitimately, that is, by organised
labour employing its resources in organising factories,
and collieries, and other producing businesses with
their own capital and at their own risk ; if a new
and better organised system of manufacture was
to replace that which is said to be oppressive and
outworn, then all honour to the suggestion.   But
this is not how the change is to come about.   Men
who have exercised no thrift, who have taken
neither responsibilities nor risks, are to take possession of what others have built up ; and it is assumed
that under this new and untried management the
industries of the country are to progress as prosper-
ously as heretofore, but that manual labour is to enjoy
the whole produce.   A more impudent proposal has
seldom or never been put forward seriously.

How Syndicalists will try to accomplish their aim
is revealed in *The Miners' Next Step*, a pamphlet
outlining the policy published during the trouble in
South Wales in the year 1912. The following
extracts from this pamphlet show the main aims
and objects :—

" *Policy.*

" i. The old policy of identity of interest between employers and ourselves be abolished and a policy of open hostility installed.

" x. Lodges should as far as possible discard the old method of coming out on strike for any little minor grievance, and adopt the more scientific weapon of the irritation strike by simply remaining at work, reducing their output, and so contrive by their general conduct to make the colliery unproductive.

" xiii. That a continual agitation be carried on in favour of increasing the minimum wage and shortening the hours of work until we have extracted the whole of the employers' profits.

" xiv. That our objective be to build up an organisation that will ultimately take over the mining industry, and carry it on in the interests of the workers."

" *The Use of the Irritation Strike.*

" Pending the publication of a pamphlet which will deal in a comprehensive and orderly way with different methods and ways of striking, the following brief explanation must suffice : The irritation strike depends for its successful adoption on the men holding clearly the point of view that their interests and the employers' are necessarily hostile. Further, that the employer is vulnerable only in one place—his profits ! Therefore, if the men wish to bring effective pressure to bear, they must use methods which tend to reduce profits. One way of doing this is to decrease production while continuing at work. Quite a number of instances where this method has been successfully adopted in South Wales could be adduced. The following will serve as an example :—

" At a certain colliery some years ago the management desired to introduce the use of screens for checking small coal. The men, who were paid through and through for coal-getting, *e.g.* for large and small coal in gross, objected, as they saw in this the thin end of the wedge of a move to reduce their earnings. The management persisted, and the men, instead of coming out on strike, reduced their output by half. Instead of sending four trams of coal from a stall, two only were filled, and so on. The management thus saw its output cut in half, while its running expenses remained the same. A few days' experience of a profitable industry turned into a losing one ended in the men winning hands down."

Here, then, is the policy in all its nakedness, and in all its impudence—a policy which the sterling good sense of the Trade Union Congress emphatically condemned in September 1912. But it has its adherents and its leaders, and already there have been attempts to make a practical trial of it ; although its success could have but one result—the material, moral and political ruin of this country.

Happily there is a better way. The improvement of the condition of labour and of the mass of the nation can be obtained—is being obtained—by a healthier and wiser policy. The labour force of a country is in its essence one and indivisible : it includes all those engaged in the work of production, from the man whose brain organises, to the boy whose hand fetches and carries. This is the first point that Socialists and Syndicalists should realise. In that labour force there are elements of varying capacity and worth—a second point to realise. It is clearly unjust that men of all capacities should receive an equal award ; as unjust as that a man of inferior capacity should hold a superior position. In the harmoniously working community of the future (to whose advent one confidently looks) each man would rise to that position he was qualified by nature, character, and his own efforts to occupy. This would be a system of justice. It would also recognise the spheres and rights of the factors in production. Land, apart from questions of ownership, would receive the rent to which its position or fertility entitled it. Capital—that is, the wealth

devoted to industrial purposes—accumulated by
thrift and abstinence, would be available for the
labour force, which would pay the rightful interest for its use.   Without this, wealth will not be
accumulated and the community will suffer.

To put it shortly, the system under which industry
has hitherto worked has been, and is, defective ; its
comparatively recent origin, its lack of precedents, or
experience to go back upon, have led to many mistakes
being made—but that on the whole the system was
sound is proved by its capability for improvement ;
it is elastic, and it is progressive.   Its defects have
been noted and remedies have been tried with success.
Its very successes have caused an impatience for
greater progress and a quicker pace towards per-
fection.   The introduction of class warfare and
irritation can only prevent progress and slow down
the pace.   An ignorance of economic laws or a
foolish opposition to their working has the same
effect.   This is the lesson that the working classes
to their honour are learning ; they can see hope,
and they realise that a bright future depends on
steady evolution rather than on stormy revolution.
A broad outlook, a knowledge of history, a compari-
son of the condition of labour to-day with that of a
century or even of half a century ago, strengthens this
feeling.   A knowledge of the advantage of working
for a skilful rather than an incompetent organiser

H

impresses its own lesson, and proves the value of the organiser's skill. Acquaintance with Economics, teaching a knowledge of the truth about wages, profits, interest, and rent, is giving a growing number of people a hopeful future for which to strive. The hopeless days of the Iron Law of Wages are over, and it is becoming increasingly evident to the mass of the population that thrift, not waste ; good organisation, not revolutionary chatter ; harmony, not friction ; a freedom to rise to the position to which a man's abilities entitle him, not the seizing of the instruments of production, are the essentials for the material well-being of every Englishman, and the continuance of our Empire.

APPENDIX A

French Delegate's Address

(Printed by permission.)

M. Jouhaux said : Comrades,—In bringing you
the fraternal greetings of the French working classes
who are grouped in the General Confederation of
French Workers, allow me first of all to join with
you in expressing our deepest sympathy in respect
of the misfortune which has happened to the English
proletariat through the events which have taken
place in Dublin.

In England, as in France and Germany, it is
always the proletariat which pays with its liberty
and its blood for any advances and conquests which
have been brought about.

The repression of the working classes by Capital
is an international factor, and the fight of the
working classes against this oppression likewise should
be an international one.

I rejoice to see the international bonds of solidarity,
of mutual interest becoming stronger day by day,
bringing the different movements and endeavours
of the workers' associations up to one level and to
one combined purpose. This is a sure sign that

" race-hatred " and the " barriers " of nationality
are fast disappearing in the ranks of the workers,
making place for a sentiment of International
Brotherhood which, in its development, will prove
the real reason for the disappearance of wars, which
always have been, and always must be, fraught
with dire consequences to the future of the international proletariat.

War, whatever the causes may be which produce
it, for the working classes has always been, and will
be, an occasion for sorrow and misery. A war always
is a set-back to the progress of civilisation. For
this reason, then, we should not hesitate to make
a stand against it. To combat the possibility of
future wars all available means ought to be considered as serving the purpose well if they will
prevent the horrors and sufferings of future wars.

The General Federation of French Workers has
never failed to smooth out any international complications which have arisen. Let us recall the
serious tension which existed in the year 1900
between the English and the French nations ; that
between France and Germany in 1911 ; the Balkan
War in 1912 ; and lastly the campaign which we
have waged in France against the reintroduction
of the three years of military service.

The Government has revenged itself by inflicting
heavy terms of imprisonment upon those of our

members who have been recognised as ardent advocates of anti-militarism. It is not, however, by such repression that the work of our Trade Unions will be turned aside, for to us they represent not only the fulfilment of our corporate desires, but a mission more largely humane—to realise the liberty of Labour by the suppression of the official and employer classes.

The immediate results are of the greatest importance to us, as they will show how to procure for the worker an increased liberty and better conditions. They will instil in the hearts of the workers the desire for a larger share of this world's goods, and will constitute that stimulus which is required to incite the workers to act in unison to secure for them their proper share of the general welfare.

We desire that the Trade Unionist should be a progressive factor in our social status ; he has been trained that, even if he be a passive factor to-day, he becomes an active factor to-morrow, and our endeavours are directed towards developing in him the principles of direct action, which is a characteristic of our form of industrial disputes.

We are of opinion that only through their own personal efforts and endeavours will the workers be able to bring about any improvements.

Only by the development and use of their strength which their occupation affords them can they realise their hopes. They should never surrender their weapons.

Direct action is opposed to the renunciation of personal effort characterised by permanent delegation by which the power of the determining value and creative force for all progress and conquests is consigned to a small number.

It is for the worker to retain for himself the mastery of the hour when his personal effort, blended in the general effort of his fellow-workers or his class, will become effective. It is the expression, so to speak, and confirmation of history—history which tells us that real progress has been deliberately realised by persistent preliminary work, of missionary enterprise, and organisation. Direct action condemns the indolence and indifference common in every individual, to whatever class he may belong. Every one of them, as a fact, accustoms himself only too easily to leave the actual effort to others, or to a power outside his own volition ; it is opposed to the comfortable state in which he looks to immobilise himself, to Providence for the realisation of his desires and wishes.

Many workers rely upon more active and bolder comrades, whose cares and efforts are centred in obtaining for these self-same colleagues of the workshop better wages and conditions, while the farmer, the merchant, the industrial magnate expect from the State such measure of protection as will secure them peace and success in their enterprises. This is on the part of every one of them a sign of barren incompetence, a proof of want of courage, and a lack of initiative.

Any class of persons incapable of acting on their own behalf, or for those around them, fully deserves to fail.

All the virtue of direct action is contained in this, that it proves to be a reaction against our usual practices, and shows us once more the exception— the exception that proves the rule. That exception we discover in the upheavals of history, where, to all appearances, the laborious care of preparation is succeeded by some sudden, and, it may be, abortive revolution. We find it too in the immense changes brought about by a wave of passion. But these passions and this agitation too soon extinguished, often amid disorganisation and incoherence, are responsible for the set-backs and disappointments which mark our tardy progress.

Thanks to the centralisation by which it can organise and co-ordinate these fleeting outbreaks of passion and discontent, Syndicalism is able to substitute conscious and continuous action.

Without doubt the worker in his task of organisation, and his struggle to secure those rights which properly belong to his class, is moved by divers aspirations ; his action sometimes is wanting in singleness of aim and the spirit of continuity ; it lacks logic ; not infrequently it reaches a state when between its practice and its theory there is a great gulf fixed. Often he is forced by circumstances to listen to dictates remote from the pretensions of his declared policy of autonomy and independence. His daily practice reveals little rectitude, and to all appearances the general tendency of *direct action* (that is known as Syndicalism) bears in itself the seeds of its own dissolution, and that the people must recognise the necessity for that permanent delegation of functions and power of reform represented by the modern State.

To appreciate this more fully, we must not fail to make due allowance for the influential power wielded by the institutions of Government and the employing classes. The force of such influences cannot be shaken off in a day, and the task is even one of greater difficulty to the working class, bruised and oppressed as it is by the pressure that is placed upon it. Syndicalism, if it compromises with the enemy, fails to recognise the legitimacy of the force which it holds in check. It is, in its essence, the negation of the employers' right. It is, for us, equally the negation of the central authority, as it is that of all organised compression and repression.

Between the employer class and the State, on the

one hand, and the wage-earners on the other, there is a state of war—of perpetual skirmishes and " guerilla " engagements, and on every occasion of conflict the stronger, for the time being, is the victor, while the weaker is overborne in the struggle.   So long as victory is for the stronger the workers must see to it that strength shall be theirs.   Till that end is achieved the proletariat must alternately impose its will and submit to compromise, which, in most cases, will never assume the form of a definite treaty.

This power which must be secured can only be acquired by the accumulation of fragmentary forces, developed, strengthened, centralised by the exercise of mind and character ; by the training of organisations in action, and perfected by the practice of self-reliance.   The weapons of the working classes are as many as they are various.   They can be applied in manifold and diverse directions, but they require, for their efficient handling, rapidity of action and ever-ready initiative.   It is in their application that the groups can demonstrate their originality, based on technical skill and the psychology of their profession ; their perspicacity and their vigour.

The economic conditions pertaining at the moment will decide the form and nature of the conflict ; whether the shock will be slight or violent

will depend on the strength of the opposing forces
and the cohesive qualities of the members of the
Union.   Nevertheless, in spite of these differences,
it will be *direct action*, so long as the interested
parties resort only to the power of their class, and
to their own will to decide for peace or for war, and
to determine what attitude shall be taken up by
their members.

Agitation, strikes, " sabotage," boycott—these
are the weapons in the hands of the workers : even
the forms themselves of *direct action*.   With each,
as with all, it is the worker alone who decides for
himself.   So, too, it is by the means at his disposal,
by his function, and his rôle that he decides the
nature of his activities and his method of fighting.

To declare a strike, the most courageous and far-
seeing members must secure the consent of all the
rest.   All must be ready for the sustained and considered effort required of each.   Success depends
upon the will-power and resistance of each individual
strike.   The result shows the amount of pressure
brought to bear on the opposing forces by the
combatants.

Sabotage demands from its authors an individual
effort, a considered act calculated to exercise an
influence on subsequent events closely allied to
the matter in hand.

The Boycott supposes that among the working

class there exists a firm determination to apply
pressure that shall deflect its members from their
accustomed habits.

An agitation of public opinion can only be created
by the personal efforts of a number of people, and
the result is measured by the sum of their personal
activity. In every case it is the worker rousing
himself to action, driven by instinct, guided by
reason, strengthened by organisation, fortified by
numerous examples, carried along by the wave,
strong in the recollection of former victories.

Success belongs to the boldest and most tenacious,
and *direct action* proceeds from boldness and tenacity.
As it is the synonym for the struggle, it exposes
every one to cuts and bruises, but it is the mani-
festation of an ever-alert will power, and the
constant protest of a working class perpetually in
motion.

A conflict thus engaged upon borrows from the
combatants the means to success ; it can repose
only upon themselves, and it is an action directly
exercised on the opposing forces. It exalts them
by developing their personal valour, by the education of their will, so that we may say even that it
transforms them.

The adversaries of the working classes do not
under-estimate the value of *direct action*. They
know that the day on which it becomes the sole

principle of the movement, their omnipotence, their reign will be over, for on that day the workers will no longer resemble a flock, of which the directing and possessing classes are the shepherds.

Then there will be a class of workers assuring its own happiness, no longer expectant of the State as an embodiment of Providence, nor of that other " Providence "—the employer class.

Happiness is not, however, a gift. It is to be won, to be achieved by *direct action*. By this method the " Confédération Générale " of France has obtained for the workers of the Republic both social and corporate benefits. To-day, in a nation of enthusiastic and ardent temperaments, more than 600,000 rebels are enrolled under its banner against the existing order of things. Opposed to these are ranged but eight organisations of workers, to whom *direct action* is unacceptable. This infinitesimal minority apart, it is the method which impels the great mass of our workers. It has welded them into unity ; it has created in them a common interest and a common aspiration which has united and coalesced the men [for] the final combat—the General Strike of Expropriation, which will replace in the hands of the workers the instruments of production.

Then, and then only, will the international workers be able to live in harmony in a society from whence militarism and the exploitation of man by man has been driven out.

Long live the International Union of Workers !

APPENDIX B

Trade Unions Congress, Manchester, 1913

GERMAN DELEGATE'S ADDRESS

(Printed by permission.)

MR CHAIRMAN, LADIES AND GENTLEMEN, FELLOW WORKERS,—The German Trade Unions have gladly accepted the kind and fraternal invitation tendered to them by your Parliamentary Committee, and they have instructed me to convey to you their hearty thanks for the invitation, and best wishes for your organisation.   They gladly accepted your invitation, not merely because they desire their delegates to transmit the German workers' brotherly greetings to our fellow-workers in the British Trade Union movement, but chiefly because they feel our presence here—at the British Parliament of Labour—will demonstrate the fact that in their thoughts and aims the Germans and British workers are one. Neither languages nor political boundaries shall keep us divided.   In spite of all those whose personal interests are in the direction of fomenting strife

between the labouring classes of our two lands,
who would even commit the crime of instigating
war, we are here to-day to loudly proclaim our
mutual, our common interests, which demand our
brotherly co-operation if we want to successfully
combat modern Capitalism. Our fight in all lands
is directed against organised capital, which is all
the better able to exploit the workers the less they
are united, and which is constantly at work in the
interests of the upper classes to keep us in the
dangers of war. We are happy to know, however,
that the working men of this country want peace,
and you may rest assured that the German workers,
too, are out for peace, and I am convinced that war
will be an impossible thing as soon as the toiling
classes of our respective countries are unanimous
on this matter.

You certainly do not expect us to give a definite
opinion on what we have seen and learned, which
is a great deal, whilst in your midst. We shall
instead, with your worthy chairman's permission,
give a brief sketch of our own movement. We do
not want you to think that by quoting these details
we wish to play the schoolmaster, but we believe
that it will interest you to have an insight into
our own methods and ideas. It is scarcely twenty
years since our fellow-unionists, full of astonishment
and admiration for your industrial movement,

almost gave up hopes of ever being able to build
up as powerful and efficient a movement as they
witnessed in your country.   By the way, conditions
as they existed at that time did not permit of us
entertaining any such hopes.   Trade Unions had
been started as early as 1865, Trade Unions which
recognised the principle of the class-war.   In 1878,
however, the so-called Anti-Socialist law was passed
which entirely did away with our organisations for
the time being.   This law was enforced in the most
brutal manner possible up to 1890, but we had, in
the meantime, commenced to reorganise, more or
less secretly, some of our trade societies.   However, there was no uniformity of any kind at that
period, and a great number of merely local unions,
or societies covering individual small trades, were
brought into being.

Immediately after the downfall of that infamous
law, we set to work earnestly and systematically
for the purpose of building up a strong and united
movement.   I think, Mr Chairman, I am not ex-
aggerating if I say that we have made the impossible
possible, and that to-day we are in no way behind
the great trade union movement of the United
Kingdom, especially if we take into consideration
the industrial development of our respective
countries.

In 1891, after the repeal of the Anti-Socialist law,

we started with a total membership of 277,659, distributed over 62 national and independent local unions. The total funds of this much too large number of unions scarcely reached the amount of £22,000. At the end of last year (1912) we had declined to 47 national unions, and there was no " localistic " union worth mentioning, while our affiliated membership had gone up to 2,559,000, including 222,300 female members. These unions report an annual income of £4,012,000, and their funds amount to £4,040,000.

Within a comparatively brief space of time we have thus succeeded in concentrating our movement, amalgamating the different trades into closely-centralised national unions, and thereby making them more powerful and effective. It would be a great mistake to believe that all this had been achieved without much opposition on the part of the Government or the employing class. Let me quote a few comparative figures : In 1890 our unions spent £52,000 on strikes and lock-outs, while in 1912 £634,000 were spent for the same purpose. In 1910 this item amounted to £980,000.

The figures just quoted are those covering the so-called General Commission of German Trade Unions, the bona-fide national centre of our industrial movement. Unfortunately, however, some of the German workers have allowed themselves to be led astray by rival unions—by the Liberal and Christian or Clerical Trade Societies.

The daily life and struggles of their unions had soon taught the German worker that Socialism— the collective ownership of all means of production and distribution—presents the only final solution of our social problems, and that, consequently, the Social Democratic Party must be their mouthpiece in the political field. The Liberal Party, as well as the Centre or political party of the Catholic Church, have, on the other hand, organised their separate unions, to be used for their various political purposes. These unions, fortunately, have never reached the importance and power they desired. The Liberal, or Hirsch-Duncker, Unions numbered 109,000 members at the beginning of this year, and 344,600 members were organised in the Christian Unions, while the total membership of all three groups amounted to 3,256,000.

These figures only relate to industrial workers ; they do not include about 800,000 clerks, shop-assistants, and similar employees who are organised in benefit societies. These societies cannot be classed with trade unions of any tendency—for they refuse to recognise the strike as a last resource in case of a dispute—otherwise we would number more than four millions of organised workers in Germany.

Many millions of agricultural workers are un-

I

organised at the present moment. Recognising the
necessity of organising these workers as well, we
have recently started to do for them what has been
done for many other trades.   Three years ago we
appointed five permanent officers for the new
National Union of Agricultural Workers, and they
were the first members of this Union which to-day
has more than 20,000 paying members. This has
been possible in spite of the fact that our agricultural
workers have been held in semi-slavery for hundreds
of years, and that they, even to-day, are subject
to the most reactionary laws and regulations.   The
National Centre of German Trade Unions, of which
Mr Legien is the president, spends about £5000 a
year on behalf of the Agricultural Workers' Union
and on behalf of a National Union of Domestic
Servants, which has been established in the same
way.   The latter union now has about 6000
members.

The class-conscious workers organised in our
unions fight for democracy on the political, or
Socialism on the industrial field.   They are, therefore, bitterly opposed by the Government and its
many allies.   Indeed, I believe there is no country
where antagonism between organised Labour and
the Government is keener than it is in Germany.
We never go to see members of the Government
and they never come to us, although out of 397

members of Parliament we have 111 Social-Demo-
crats, and out of a total vote of 11 millions cast at
the last General Election we polled more than four
millions and a quarter for the party of Labour.
Our opponents are still too strong for us, mainly
because the Liberals of our country have no desire
to help to overthrow the absolute rule of the Con-
servatives or Feudalists ; they are themselves too
much afraid of the workers.

We are, all the same, full of hope for the future.
We sincerely trust that the International Labour
movement will finally triumph over all its opponents
and obstacles.   We have to-day an international
combination of trade unions which embraces eighteen countries and seven and a half millions trade
union members, including your General Federation
of Trade Unions.   Our international co-operation is
being developed and improved year by year, teaching
the workers of all lands the necessity of getting
acquainted with each other, of learning from each
other, and of fighting for the same objects and aims.

Want of time, unfortunately, prevents me telling
you about many other aspects of our Labour movement.   Every union has its weekly paper delivered
free to all its members.   The unions of all cities
of any importance have their own Labour Temples,
attached to which are hostelries for our travelling
members, legal advice offices for the workers, the

I*

latter in charge of men from the rank and file whom
we trained at our own school. For other trade
union officers, old and young, we have a separate
school. Our political party has 90 daily papers,
printed in 62 printing establishments owned by the
Party, and in almost every case the building where
the printing plant is put up is also owned by
the Party. Our trade union papers have a circulation of about three million copies per week, and our
Socialist dailies alone have more than 1,500,000
regular subscribers. By the way, we believe a
worker to be little better than a blackleg if he sup-
ports the Capitalist Press instead of subscribing to
the paper belonging to his own class. There are
more than 7000 Socialist City and Town Councillors
in Germany, and our influence is thus felt in all
parts of public life. The Co-operative movement,
too, is developing very rapidly.

We have, after many experiences of all sorts,
learned to combine in the three fields of Labour's
struggle—in the trade unions, in our own political
party, and in the Co-operative movement. These
three movements to-day work hand in hand, and
German Labour presents a united front to its
opponents. We sincerely hope the same unity of
purpose and action will soon be brought about
among the workers of all lands. With this end
in view we have much pleasure in inviting your

Congress to send representatives to our next triennial Trade Unions Congress, which assembles in June next year. We have handed an official invitation to our friend Bowerman, the secretary of your Parliamentary Committee. A better mutual understanding among the working classes of our countries, a permanent and close co-operation of our organisations, I trust, Mr Chairman, will do much in assuring peace among our great nations, and materially assist us to build up an irresistible organisation of Labour.

We again thank you heartily for your invitation and truly British hospitality, and hope to be able to receive your delegates in our midst at the next German Trade Unions Congress.

APPENDIX C

TABLE OF FIGURES FROM "THE CASE FOR THE LABOUR PARTY : A HANDBOOK OF FACTS AND FIGURES FOR WORKERS," PAGE 58

WAGES

" By use of Index numbers the Board of Trade have compiled a return showing the course of Wages and Prices of the necessaries of life since 1850.

Fixing the rate of wages and average wholesale prices for that year at 100, Wages and Prices for subsequent years are set out in percentage of those prevailing in that year.

Year.				Wages.	Prices.
1850	.	.	.	100	100
1855	.	.	.	..	131·2
1860	.	.	.	119·2	128·6
1865	.	.	.	127·5	131·2
1870	.	.	.	134·1	124·7
1875	.	.	.	161·4	124·7
1880	.	.	.	148·8	114·3
1885	.	.	.	149·4	93·5
1890	.	.	.	161·3	93·5
1895	.	.	.	159·2	80·5
1900	.	.	.	178·7	97·4
1905	.	.	.	173·3	93·5
1906	.	.	.	175·7	100·0
1907	.	.	.	181·7	103·9 "

Note.—The Table ends at 1907. Since then *Wages* showed a decrease of one in 1908, and of the same amount in 1909 ; during 1910 and 1911 there was a slight rise of about one-half.

Prices went up two and a half between 1907 and 1908, then remained fairly stationary during 1909 ; in 1910 they rose about one and a half, since when they have tended to fall.

APPENDIX D

APPENDIX D

DIAGRAM SHOWING THE THEORY OF PROFITS IN A STAPLE INDUSTRY

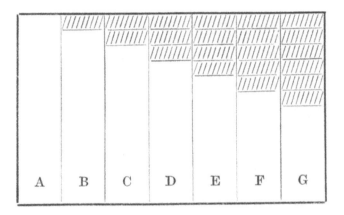

EXPLANATION :—

Block A indicates the selling price.

Blocks B to G indicate manufacturers of varying degrees of efficiency ; the shaded portions mark profits, the unshaded portions mark the cost of production—selling price being made up of cost of production *plus* profit. (*Note.*—The selling price must be at the same rate for all quantities of a staple commodity sold in the same market.)

Block B indicates what occurs in the case of the least efficient manufacturer : small amount of profit, great cost of production.

Block G indicates low cost of production, comparatively high profit made by the most efficient manufacturer—this high profit being possible owing to the inefficiency of B.

If you could restrict the industry to manufacturers of the highest efficiency (say Blocks F and G in the diagram) the cost to the buyer might be reduced to the white space in Block E—*i.e.* in this instance would be diminished by nearly one-third. Moreover, if other things remained constant, the greater output required of manufacturers of the F and G class would enable them to manufacture more cheaply—the experience in modern business being, the greater the output, the less the cost.

Note.—Generally speaking, it is the employers of the B class who are sweaters, and employ people under inferior conditions. The employers of G class have well-organised, well-equipped factories, and know the advantage of treating their workpeople well.

INDEX